W0017940

Common Kingsnakes

Plus Related Species

FROM THE EXPERTS AT
ADVANCED VIVARIUM SYSTEMS®

By David Perlowin with Jerry G. Walls

THE HERPETOCULTURAL LIBRARY®

Lead Editor Jarelle S. Stein
Consulting Editor: Russ Case
Art Director: Cindy Kassebaum
Production Supervisor: Jessica Jaensch
Production Coordinator: Leah Rosalez
Book Project Specialist: Karen Julian
Indexer: Melody Englund

Vice President, Chief Content Officer: June Kikuchi
Vice President, Kennel Club Books: Andrew DePrisco
I-5 Press: Jennifer Calvert, Amy Deputato,
Karen Julian, Jarelle S. Stein

Front cover photo by Paul Freed; back cover photo by Bill Love.
The additional photographs in this book are by Paul Freed, pp. 5–9, 11
(top), 12, 15, 17, 20, 21, 24, 25, 29, 39, 41 (bottom), 53–55, 59–66, 69,
70, 72, 73, 77, 79–81, 82, 86, 91, 94–96; Bill Love, pp. 10, 11 (bottom), 41
(top), 45, 49, 51, 67; Isabelle Francais, p. 31; James Gerholdt, pp. 85, 89.

LCCN: 96-183295
ISBN: 978-1-882770-81-6

An Imprint of I-5 Press
A Division of I-5 Publishing, LLC
3 Burroughs
Irvine, CA 92618
866-888-5526
www.avsbooks.com

Printed and bound in China
16 15 14 13 12 1 2 3 4 5 6 7 8 9 10

Contents

Foreword

Common kingsnakes (genus *Lampropeltis*), particularly the California king, are among the most popular and widely kept snakes in herpetoculture. Their beauty, moderate size, ease of maintenance, and relative docility have made kingsnakes one of the most recommended snake species for the beginning hobbyist. In addition, common kings readily breed in captivity, and a variety of subspecies, geographic variants, and color and pattern morphs have been established by both hobbyists and commercial breeders. Few snakes can match the crisp beauty and the display appeal of an outstanding desert-phase California king or the variety of colors and patterns found in these North American snakes.

The purpose of chapters 1–7 of this book is to provide essential information to novice snake keepers as well as to serious hobbyists and professional breeders interested in keeping and breeding common kingsnakes. The information comes from texts and papers, conversations with kingsnake breeders, and my own experiences.

The cooperation of Robert Applegate, Dorothy DeLisle, Chris Estep, Bill and Kathy Love, Paula Scarpellino, Vince Scheidt, and Gary Sipperly is greatly appreciated. Special thanks to Philippe de Vosjoli for all his help and hard work.

—David Perlowin

In addition to the common kings, there are seven other kingsnake species. They include a variety of strikingly colored milksnakes and mountain kings as well as the spectacular gray-banded kings and the prairie kings; the latter species is most closely related to the common king. Chapters 8–11 discuss these species. Hobbyists are fortunate that all of the species and most of the subspecies of kings are widely available and often inexpensive. The kingsnakes have something for every taste and budget.

—Jerry G. Walls

CHAPTER 1

General Information

There is a bit of a name game to play when it comes to the common kingsnake. The scientific name is *Lampropeltis getula*. The name *Lampropeltis* is derived from the Greek words *lampro*, meaning "shiny," and *peltis*, meaning "shield," no doubt referring to the glassy sheen and smooth appearance of the scales.

If you pick up a book written before about 1990, you may see the species names given as *getulus* instead of *getula*. Technically that was a mistake, as the word *Lampropeltis* is a feminine generic name and therefore requires that the species name also be feminine. Thus *getulus* (masculine) had to be changed to *getula* (feminine), as did *L. g. niger* to *L. g. nigra* and *nigritus* to *nigrita*.

What is probably of more interest to today's hobbyists than that bit of history, however, is the seemingly constant changing of status between species and subspecies. Is

The California kingsnake is one of the most popular captive-bred king-snakes in the reptile trade today. The species is available in many types of morphs, such as the 50-50 shown here.

it *Lampropeltis getula holbrooki* or *Lampropeltis holbrooki*, for instance? Currently all the North American reptiles are being investigated with new technological methods, especially those used in molecular genetics, and the results often change well-established usage. As the changes have not yet been accepted by all specialists, this book has tried to steer a middle course, using traditional names but trying to let readers know that changes are probably coming.

Distribution

Common kingsnakes have a widespread North American distribution, ranging from southern New Jersey to Florida in the East, across the central plains states, and into the Southwest. They are also found in the West from southern Oregon down to northern Mexico. Kingsnakes inhabit a range of environments, including deserts, farmlands, prairies, riverbanks, and deciduous forests as well as pine forests. Kingsnakes can be found anywhere there is an abundance of rodents (barns, for example).

Where to Find Common Kings for Pets

The most frequently offered wild-collected common kingsnakes are the Florida kingsnake, the eastern kingsnake, and the speckled kingsnake. Most of the other kingsnakes now

This speckled kingsnake has a high-contrast pattern—a trait that makes this species desirable.

The black kingsnake (*L. getula nigra*) has not achieved much popularity in the trade because of its lack of color, its faded pattern, and its aggressive temperament.

available to the public are captive-bred and sold to reptile wholesalers or directly to specialty stores. The most popular of these are the California kingsnake, its various morphs, and the albino speckled kingsnake. For those able to attend any of the reptile expos and sales that occur with regularity around the country, all of the subspecies (an exception may be the Outer Banks kingsnake) and most of the variants of common kingsnakes are available as captive-bred hatchlings. Many of the adult kingsnakes available are wild-caught, although some may be either "old breeders" from a reptile breeder's overstock or captive-raised pets that owners no longer want to keep. It is a good idea to inquire about the origin and age of an animal before purchasing it.

Size

Common kingsnake hatchlings range from 6 inches (15 cm) for runts to 13 inches (33 cm). Adults measure from 36 inches (91 cm) in speckled kings (*L. g. holbrooki*) to 60 inches (1.5 m) in California kings (*L. g. californiae*) and Florida kings (*L. g. floridana*) to 84 inches (2.1 m) in eastern kingsnakes (*L. g. getula*).

Sexing

Immature kingsnakes do not demonstrate any obvious sexual characteristics. Hatchlings and subadults are best sexed either through manual eversion of the hemipenes or with the use of sexing probes. Adult kingsnakes usually show a

Shown here are a female (*top*) and a male (*bottom*) albino California kingsnake. Note the male's thicker tail base.

A professional inserts a sexing probe into this Brook's kingsnake. If the probe reaches a depth of seven subcaudal scales, it is an indication that this snake is male.

By manually everting the hemipenis in this Brook's kingsnake, you can tell it's a male. Lack of an everted hemipene indicates a snake is either female or a male with extremely strong muscles at the hemipenal bases.

marked difference in the degree of tail taper past the vent. The tails of males, because they contain the inverted hemipenes, will appear markedly thicker at their bases and not taper as sharply as do the tails of females. If you're in doubt about the sex of a kingsnake, consult a breeder or a veterinarian to manually sex your snake or use a sexing probe to avoid injuring the snake.

Pattern and Color Variations

There is some variation of skin color and pattern within all subspecies of common kingsnakes, but none demonstrates more distinct morphs than the California kingsnake, which ranks as one of the most variable of all snakes, and the blotched kingsnake (*L. g. "goini"*). In terms of pattern variation in common kingsnakes, one finds in herpetoculture an emphasis on breeding for such desirable traits as width of banding and definition of pattern. In California kingsnakes, herpetoculturists emphasize width of striping, asymmetrical patterning, broken patterning, or reduction of pattern (as in the 90 percent yellow California kingsnakes, also marketed as banana kings). In other subspecies of kingsnakes, herpetoculturists focus on pattern definition or pattern reduction. For example, a clean, clearly defined, high-contrast pattern will be emphasized by

The reduced black pigmentation of this juvenile hypomelanistic Brook's kingsnake makes this species an eye-catcher.

This sharp-looking hatchling is a blaze-phase blotched kingsnake.

aficionados of the beautiful desert kingsnake. A reduction of dark patterning will be sought by herpetoculturists seeking to produce high-quality golden-phase (or "brooksi") morphs of the Florida kingsnake. As should be evident from the information presented so far, California kingsnakes, because of their phenotypic variability, rank among the best candidates for genetic studies on pattern and color in snakes.

The most popular and widely produced color morphs of the common kingsnake are amelanistic (lacking black

A Note on Subspecies

Quotation marks appear around subspecies that herpetologists no longer recognize taxonomically but that are still recognized as a phase by hobbyists and dealers in herpetoculture. (Herpetoculturists are interested in keeping and breeding reptiles and amphibians of all types for both personal goals and commercial purposes, while herpetologists study reptiles and amphibians from a more scientific view and are not necessarily interested in keeping them in captivity or breeding them. Some herpetologists are, of course, herpetoculturists.)

Shown here is a juvenile Brook's kingsnake (also called the south Florida kingsnake) displaying a reduced dark pattern, which is more prominent in true Florida kingsnakes.

pigmentation) albino California and speckled kingsnakes. In the California kingsnake, the coastal phase (brown and yellow) and desert phase (black and white) are selectively bred to emphasize these characteristics. In other kingsnake subspecies, color morphs are also being selectively bred, such as the black and orange phase of the blotched kingsnake. There also are a few anerythristic (lacking red pigmentation) south Florida kingsnakes currently in captivity that should eventually become more available. Additional

Crossing the albino trait with other pattern and color variations has led to new remarkable morphs, such as this lavender albino speckled king.

Among captive-bred species, albino California kings, as shown here, are widely available specimens.

color and pattern morphs are expected to become available because of the large-scale efforts to commercially breed common kingsnakes.

Albino Kingsnakes

Several specimens of albino kingsnakes have been collected from the wild and have formed the foundation for the large numbers of albino kingsnakes now produced in captivity. Currently, albinos of two subspecies, the California kingsnake and speckled kingsnake, are commercially bred on a large scale. More recently, an albino black kingsnake (*L. g. nigra*) has been produced in captivity. There are several genetic lines of albino California kingsnakes currently established in captivity and characterized by variations in eye color (e.g., ruby-eyed) and skin color (e.g., lavender). The albino trait has been introduced into most other color and pattern morphs of the California kingsnake. This has led to interesting morphs, such

This albino California king carries the ruby-eye trait.

as the albino desert-phase striped California kingsnake and the recently developed snow king, which resulted from introducing the albino trait into the chocolate (patternless) morph of the California kingsnake. A solid lemon yellow albino is but a few years ahead. In terms of breeding, the albino trait is considered and dealt with as a simple recessive trait.

Herpetocultural Trends

When it comes to color and pattern, the herpetocultural trend is toward crisp, well-defined patterns and clean, contrasting colors. There is not much interest in developing genetic lines of cryptic, murkily colored kingsnakes. Thus, pure black animals are often considered more desirable than animals that are black with even a suggestion of underlying pattern. Desert kingsnakes with crisp, clearly defined bands are more desirable than those with a less distinct pattern. At a color level, the trend is toward pure colors—pure white and pure yellow are preferred to creamy yellow and off-white. (You'll find a more detailed discussion of kingsnake subspecies and their color variations in chapter 8.)

Growth Rate and Longevity in Captivity

Fortunately for kingsnake owners, the moderate growth rate and ultimate size of kingsnakes are such that they will not quickly outgrow cage space or pose handling problems. Snakes raised in captivity and in ideal conditions can reach adult size in less than three years, by which time they should be able to breed. If maintained and fed properly, hatchling kingsnakes should double in length and girth during their first year and achieve at least a further doubling of length and girth by the end of the second year. Thus, a California kingsnake that is 9 inches (23 cm) at hatching should be 18 inches (46 cm) after the first year and at least 36 inches (91 cm) after the second year.

The longevity of common kingsnakes has largely become a measure of vastly improved husbandry techniques. The average life expectancy of a common kingsnake kept in optimal captive conditions ranges from ten to fifteen years. The maximum longevity up to this point for a captive common kingsnake is twenty-three years.

CHAPTER 2

Selection

Research federal and state laws that may regulate the keeping of common kingsnakes in your area. Do not rely on legal information from pet store employees or dealers at an expo; they may be unaware of the laws that pertain to you. Most state laws do not differentiate between wild-caught and captive-bred animals, although some states, such as California and Indiana, allow albino variants of otherwise protected species or subspecies. Several states (such as Georgia and Ohio) and cities (such as Chicago and New York City) prohibit the commercial sale of native kingsnake species or subspecies, so be sure that you are informed of all of the local laws.

There is no doubt that a captive-bred kingsnake is one of the best selections for a novice snake keeper. A wild-caught kingsnake, by contrast, can be difficult to handle and may have health problems that require extensive treatment. So when purchasing a wild-caught kingsnake, take your time, don't rush the process. In fact, even though many different captive-bred varieties of kingsnakes are available and normally quite healthy, all snakes should be examined carefully before purchase. The following guidelines will help you select potentially healthy snakes.

1. Before handling a potential acquisition, visually inspect the snake. Check to see that the body is well rounded with no outlines of the ribs or backbone showing. Check to see that there are no depressions along the sides indicative of broken ribs. Check the skin for sores and scabs that may indicate that the snake either was roughly handled when collected or transported or has been kept in poor conditions. While the snake is still resting in its enclosure, look

Shown here is a Burmese python with body trauma. Do not purchase a snake with cuts or sores; raised scales indicate possible infection.

to see whether it periodically opens its mouth as if it is having trouble breathing. This could indicate some sort of respiratory problem, possibly an infection or parasites. Avoid gaping snakes.

2. Have the snake handed to you. A healthy kingsnake, whether wild-caught or captive-bred, should feel strong and give an impression of good muscle tone when handled. Wild-caught kingsnakes tend to work their way out of your hands and, when they're about halfway clear, start wagging their bodies back and forth in big sweeps to get free. This may not seem like an endearing behavior, but it certainly demonstrates a kingsnake's muscular vigor. Avoid snakes that are sluggish and limp. This invariably indicates poor health.

3. With the snake still in hand, you can perform a number of other steps to determine health. First, have someone assist you by firmly holding the body of the snake while you hold the snake behind its head. Partially open the mouth of the snake either by applying light downward pressure to the side of the lower jaw using your thumb or by gently pulling down on the skin under the snake's lower jaw. This is best done one side at a time. Look for an unusual amount of mucus in the mouth. Search for any red spots, lesions, or accumulations of caseous

material (cheesy-looking matter) along the gumline and tooth line. The presence of abundant or bubbly mucus is a reliable indicator of a respiratory infection. The red spots most likely indicate the beginning of stomatitis (mouth rot). The cheesy-looking matter is a sure sign of advanced stomatitis. Do not purchase snakes with these symptoms.

4. While still holding the head, check the eyes to make sure that they are clear and free of any signs of cloudiness, damage, or injuries. If the snake happens to be in shed, both eyes should have the same amount of cloudiness or blue tones. It may be a good idea to wait until after the snake has shed to complete your examination.

5. Allow the snake to slide between your hands. Using your fingertips, gently feel for unusual indentations or lumps along the body. Do not purchase snakes with these problems.

6. Check the underside (belly) of the snake for stained, damaged, or raised scales. These are probable signs of skin infections. Do not purchase any snake with these symptoms.

7. Mites are a common problem in snakes, whether wild-caught or captive-bred. Thoroughly check any prospective addition to your collection for these external parasites. Look for beadlike mites crawling on the snake or tiny silvery white specks scattered over the body (these specks are mite feces). Next, check the edges of the eyes where mites can be imbedded between the rim and the eye itself. The presence of mites gives a raised impression to the eye rim. After looking for mites on the snake, closely inspect your hands to see if any tiny beadlike creatures are crawling about. The treatment of these parasites is never easy on the snake, and the mites can readily spread throughout your collection. So unless you are in need of that particular snake, you would do best to avoid an infected specimen. (See chapter 6 for mite treatment.)

8. Check for ticks. These are also external parasites, although they are much larger than mites. They look like flattened, round, nearly scalelike organisms that attach themselves between the scales almost anywhere on the body. They are not the life-threatening problem mites are, but they should be removed as soon as possible when you get home.

9. Inspect around the opening to the cloaca (vent). Make sure the anal scale lies flat, is undamaged, and is free of any crusty substance. Check that there is no smeared fecal matter on the surrounding area.

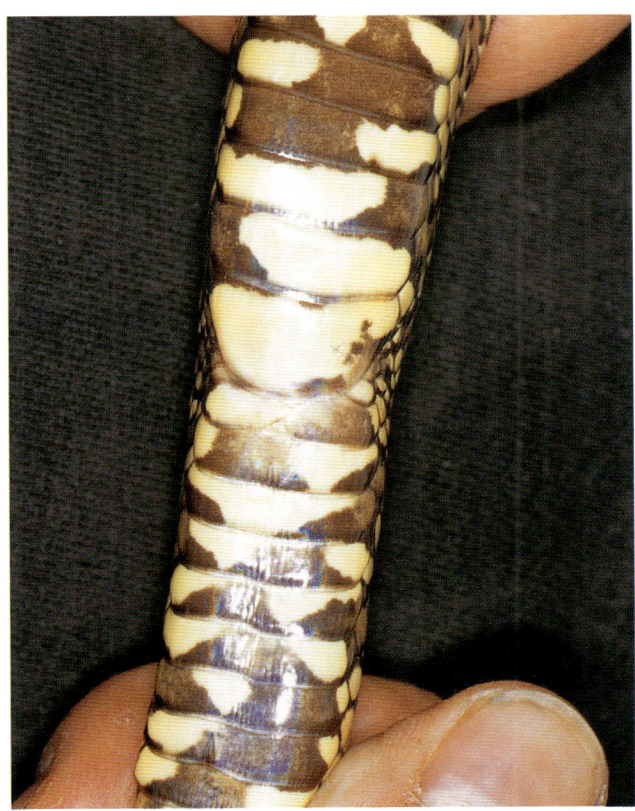

Before purchasing a snake, inspect the cloacal opening. This healthy kingsnake's vent is free of crusty matter, and the anal scale lies flat.

CHAPTER 3

Initial Care
and Handling

When you bring your new kingsnake home, you should place it in an appropriate escape-proof enclosure with heat gradients, a water dish, and a shelter (see chapter 4). These, of course, should be purchased well before your snake needs them. If you already have a collection, put the newcomer in a quarantine situation, placing its enclosure in a separate room. Newly purchased snakes brought into an established collection could pose a serious health threat to the other reptiles. The quarantine period should last from eight to twelve weeks, depending on the health of the snake.

Except for a parasite treatment or cage cleaning, leave the kingsnake alone for two to three days. The snake shouldn't be handled until it shows clear signs of adapting to captivity (feeding, gaining and maintaining weight, and being vigorous when active). Wild-caught kingsnakes will acclimate to captive conditions within a relatively short time, although there can be many exceptions. The great majority of captive-bred kingsnakes will readily feed and adjust to their new homes.

Quarantine

Ideally, you should quarantine the new snake in a different room using disinfected enclosures that you can easily clean and monitor. Newspaper is the best substrate for this purpose. The tools that you employ for all tasks, such as cleaning, related to the quarantine cage and its occupant should only be used for them. In fact, it is a good idea to restrict tools to one animal and one cage.

If you do need to use tools with other animals and cages, the tools must be dipped in a safe disinfectant designed for use with reptiles, which can be purchased at a pet shop or through your veterinarian. Do not transfer food items, cage furniture, and such from one cage to another without thoroughly disinfecting them first.

Remember your own hygiene as well. Use disposable latex gloves, if possible, or at least use disinfectant after working on quarantined cages. Always wash with a disinfectant soap such as povidone-iodine (brand name Betadine) scrub after maintenance of animals. A good maintenance protocol is to deal with animals in the quarantine area only at the end of the day, when you will not need to return to your established collection.

Initial Health Care

With wild-collected snakes, it is highly recommended that a reptile veterinarian perform a stool check for parasites. Obtain an estimate from a veterinarian as to the cost for a parasite check. In some cases, veterinarians will charge an amount several times the cost of the snake for a thorough parasite check and treatment. If the cost is too high, consider a routine treatment for at least nematodes and flagellate protozoans. Most wild-caught snakes tend to be infested with at least one type of internal parasite that must be treated immediately. These may include nematodes (roundworms), trematodes (flukes), cestodes (tapeworms), pentastomes (tongue worms), and protozoans.

If you don't have a reptile veterinarian, then your regular veterinarian should at least be able to determine the general type of internal parasites that may be infecting your kingsnake and the best course of treatment for it. If you can't afford this treatment or just don't want to pay for it, then selecting a wild-caught snake is probably not the best course of action.

Any ticks should be removed as soon as possible by applying a drop of rubbing alcohol to the body of the tick. After a few minutes, firmly pull out the tick with a pair of tweezers. Although Lyme disease is not known to be carried by these ticks, exercise safety by wearing disposable gloves.

After the initial settling-in period, proceed with the feeding steps described in chapter 5.

Handling

A principal appeal of common kingsnakes, both captive-bred and wild-caught, is their docile dispositions. Adult wild-caught common kingsnakes need to be handled often and on a consistent basis to keep them easily manageable. Wild-caught adults often tend to produce foul-smelling musk when first collected, but with repeated handling, they usually stop performing this offensive behavior.

The speckled kingsnake is one subspecies of the common kingsnake that, when collected, often exhibits defensive behavior. When handled, this subspecies consistently coils and strikes while vigorously rattling its tail. It takes determined effort and regular gentle handling by a snake keeper to habituate a nervous, aggressive snake to handling. Fortunately, when speckled kingsnakes are obtained as captive-bred hatchlings or subadults, regular gentle handling usually eliminates any aggressive behavior. California kingsnakes also have a reputation of being nippy initially.

Speckled kingsnakes, such as the one seen here, are often extremely defensive, and it may take some time before they get used to being handled. They're known to coil, strike, and rattle their tails when nervous. So be patient with a newly acquired speckled king and careful in your handling.

Adult kingsnakes grow to about 5 feet (1.5 m) long—even longer in some species, including the eastern king. Handle your snake with both hands to provide the proper support, and allow the snake to move between your hands without restraining it.

Common kingsnakes move in a persistent and determined manner. Handling a subadult or an adult requires the use of both hands to support the snake without trying to restrain its movements, essentially allowing it to move from hand to hand. Eventually, the snake should calm down, and you will be able to handle it with ease.

Hatchlings tend to always be in motion, and the safest way to handle them is with open hands for brief periods of time (no more than five minutes), preferably over a tabletop to prevent their falling to the floor. Once hatchlings get some size (especially girth) to them, regular, gentle handling can occur more frequently. When handling any snake, regardless of type, never let it coil around your neck or get near your face.

Sometimes a common kingsnake will become agitated when being handled and will perform the typical flight movements, whereby it violently swings its body back and forth. If the snake does display this type of behavior, it is best to return it to its cage and try again another time. Using excessive restraint when a snake performs this flight behavior can sometimes cause injuries.

CHAPTER 4

Housing and Maintenance

Kingsnakes should be housed in enclosures specifically made for snakes. These include several different types of commercially constructed enclosures of either all glass with sliding screen tops, all fiberglass with sliding glass fronts that can be locked, or custom-made wooden cages with framed glass or Plexiglas doors that can also be locked.

Selecting an Enclosure

Some professional colubrid breeders use a custom-built cage that has two separate compartments. The upper compartment has a water dish and one or two shelters and can be accessed through a front-opening, locking, framed glass door. The bottom compartment is a drawer that the snake can enter through a hole cut in the bottom of the upper compartment. This lower compartment acts as a hiding place and allows ease of cleaning. With this setup, pairs can readily be kept together. During feeding, each snake is relegated to its own compartment by plugging the hole connecting the compartments.

An alternative to the above-mentioned cage is to keep kingsnakes in large plastic storage containers of appropriate size (see pages 23–24), which some commercial breeders use. These are placed on shelving that is spaced in such a way as to allow no space between the top of the plastic lid and the bottom of the shelf above it. This rack system allows for relatively inexpensive housing with good security against escapes. The keys to this system are spacing the shelves correctly and making sure the width of the shelf is at least as wide as the lid of the container. Of course, every container housing a snake must have a shelf above it. For

Be Responsible

There is an ever-growing trend in local government to restrict the ownership of all exotic animals, including reptiles. Every time a snake escapes and other people become aware of it, more weight is added to the arguments of those favoring restrictions. Think of neighbors who, if confronted with a snake, may overreact (by taking a shovel to the poor animal, then reporting the incident to authorities, for example). Act responsibly, for all snake keepers and their snakes, by getting a cage with a proper locking mechanism.

adult kingsnakes, large plastic containers (26 quart [25 L]) are recommended. Adequate ventilation is critical, so make sure that several holes are drilled in each side (for softer, semitranslucent plastic containers) or burned through using a soldering iron (for hard, clear plastic containers). Hard plastic containers can easily crack if you use a drill. If you use a soldering iron, make sure you are in a well-ventilated area, and avoid breathing any fumes.

Cages that are not specifically made to house snakes, such as all-glass aquaria with separate screen tops, are not escape-proof and therefore are not recommended for most snakes, including kingsnakes, which are extremely good escape artists. (Adding locking clips designed for screen tops helps, but it does not prevent all escapes.) So be responsible and obtain the proper enclosure or build one to suit your needs. Do not make the selection of an enclosure secondary to your purchase of a snake. There are hundreds, if not thousands, of stories of pet snakes escaping from inadequate enclosures.

Size of the Enclosure

Dimensions for the housing of hatchling kingsnakes should be no smaller than 12 inches long, 6 inches wide, and 3 inches deep (30 cm x 15 cm x 7.5 cm). This size corresponds

This enclosure's top screen is secured with locking clips.

to the size of a 2-quart (1.9-L) plastic container, which is also secure enough for juvenile kingsnakes.

For small adults, a 10-gallon (38-L) aquarium (20 inches x 10 inches [51 x 25 cm]) with a locking screen top (not just locking clips) works well and is widely available in most pet stores. This size enclosure will work for most king-snakes up to one year old. A 16-quart (15-L) plastic storage container is also a good size for small adults.

For adult kingsnakes, the minimum size enclosure should be 24 inches (61 cm) long and 11 inches (28 cm) wide, which corresponds to a 20-gallon (76-L) aquarium. Larger species need a 30 inches x 12 inches (76 cm x 30 cm) or larger enclosure.

If you want more than the strictly utilitarian enclosure, there is the option of designing a naturalistic vivarium. Vivaria of 29 gallons (110 L) or more are recommended for this purpose. With a more natural type of substrate, such as pieces of cork bark or driftwood, and possibly one of the various natural-looking shelters, you can create an attractive vivarium.

Substrate

There are several substrates widely used for kingsnakes. Butcher paper and newspaper have very distinct advantages: they are cheap, somewhat absorbent, readily available, and very easy to change when soiled. They aren't attractive, but they are functional. During the acclimation stage, kingsnakes should be kept on paper so you can more easily monitor their stools and detect mites and treat the snakes.

Once you are sure that the snake is acclimated, you can use other substrate materials. One popular choice is shredded aspen, which is sold in bulk as small-animal bedding. Certain types of wood shavings (such as cedar and redwood) that may contain harmful compounds should be avoided. Some snake keepers have suggested that even pine shavings are potentially harmful because they can become lodged in a snake's mouth when the snake is fed, possibly causing mouth problems. Keep a close watch for this problem. Food should be dry when fed, which lowers the chance of bits of substrate adhering to the body of the prey.

Number 3 aquarium gravel (which is a smooth, fine, rounded gravel, not silica sand) makes an attractive, natural-looking, and easily changeable substrate. Other herpetoculturists have chosen to use a fine grade aquarium silica sand,

Newspaper makes a good substrate for quarantine enclosures. It's easy to replace and relatively inexpensive.

which can be attractive in naturalistic desert-type vivaria. Europeans have successfully used sand-soil mixes. Early herpetoculturists had poor success keeping snakes on soil because the soil's surface was kept wet and it tended to cause dangerous skin blisters and even death. If you design your vivarium so that a significant portion of the upper crust of the soil is dry, then you shouldn't experience a problem with this type of substrate. This is similar to what happens in the wild in many areas where the sun essentially dries out the soil surface. The bottom line is that most snakes will not fare well if kept for prolonged periods on a damp substrate.

Heating

Common kingsnakes have such a wide distribution that generalized temperature ranges may at first seem inappropriate. The key is to provide a temperature gradient; this allows a snake to select the temperature that suits it best. A temperature gradient of 77°F–86°F (25°C–30°C) will be suitable for all common kingsnakes. Many kingsnake specialists feel that it is very important for the optimal health of the snakes to provide a well-defined gradient. The nighttime temperature can be allowed to drop into the mid- to low 70s F (low 20s C).

There are several types of reptile heaters now available that will work for kingsnakes. These include reptile heating pads that are either placed inside the cage or attached to the underside and heating strips with built-in or added-on thermostatic controls. Because kingsnakes are rather secretive animals, incandescent light bulbs and fixtures are inappropriate and should not be used. Avoiding these lights also eliminates the possibility of thermal burns, which happen all too often with incandescent heating.

It is essential that a thermometer be used to calibrate the cage temperature, regardless of which heating system is used. This will ensure that the surface area where the heat source is located is not too hot (the highest temperature should be 86°F [30°C]). You can use several different types of thermometers. The best available are electronic digital thermometers with an external probe that can be placed directly over the heat source of the enclosure. An inexpensive alternative is to use two of the adhesive strip–type (LCD) thermometers, placing one on the cool end and the other on the warm end. Unfortunately, you will get a reading of only the air temperature in the enclosure and not a direct reading from the heat source.

Do not under any circumstance use hot rocks without some way of controlling the heat output (such as a rheostat or thermostat). Some of the hot rock- or hot block-type heaters can burn you as well as your snake. If these heating devices are not used properly, they can cause thermal burns that could seriously injure the snake as well as run up big veterinary bills. The surface temperature of some hot rocks reaches 105°F (41°C). Recently, hot rock-type heaters have been developed with thermostatic controls. Inquire about such products at your local pet store.

Shelters

Kingsnakes are relatively secretive animals. In the wild, they tend to hide during the greater part of the day; they exhibit similar behavior in captivity. An exception to this is during the breeding season, when the snakes may be out looking for mates. Appropriate shelters must be provided to restrict the amount of light and give the snakes a sense of confinement. Two shelters should be placed in the vivarium—one in the warm area and one in the cool area.

There are now many different kinds of reptile shelters available in the pet trade that will work for kingsnakes. A natural and attractive shelter can be made from curled sections of cork bark, which you can purchase from pet stores, reptile dealers, and sometimes plant nurseries. Some people use cardboard boxes and tubes, which will work but tend to be unsightly and disintegrate quickly. Cardboard is also easily moved around by the snake itself, thus removing any sense of solidity and security. There are attractive molded plastic, formed concrete, and natural wood shelters now offered in the pet trade that work well.

CHAPTER 5

Feeding

Kingsnakes feed on a variety of warm-blooded prey (such as mice and small rats) and cold-blooded prey (such as lizards, other snakes, and even hatchling turtles). Because kingsnakes are snake eaters, each must be kept separate in its own cage when young. Problems with cannibalism are most likely to occur with hatchlings and subadults. This problem diminishes when the snakes are full-grown adults. However, it has been noted that desert-dwelling kingsnakes are more prone to eat other snakes. In the deserts, there tend to be fewer rodents and more naturally occurring small species of snakes than there are in the cooler, more humid climates on the coasts, which provide a better habitat for rodents. This may explain why desert-dwelling species are more prone to cannibalism.

An interesting aspect of kingsnake feeding habits is the fact that because kingsnakes are immune to the venom of native American pit vipers—the rattlesnakes (*Sistrurus* spp. and *Crotalus* spp.), copperheads (*Agkistrodon* spp.), and allies—they may include the vipers in their natural diet. Kingsnakes are one of the very few types of snakes that exhibit this immunity. Regardless of prey type captured, kingsnakes usually kill prey by constricting it, pressing it against a hard surface, or both.

Feeding Hatchlings

Feeding captive-bred hatchlings is normally no problem. Many kingsnake breeders sell their hatchlings only after they have started feeding. Hatchling kingsnakes usually start to feed a few days to a few weeks after the first shed (some start before shedding). Make sure that each snake is housed separately and that each is provided with a shelter and a small container of water.

The best, most convenient initial food item for a hatchling is a one- to two-day-old mouse. One nice feature of keeping common kingsnakes of all sizes in captivity is that, in general,

This young speckled king gobbles up a pinky mouse. Your hatchling and subadult species will usually take one or two mice every two to seven days.

they will readily feed on prekilled mice, whether fresh or frozen. Frozen pinkies (newborn mice), fuzzies (eyes closed, but hair starting to grow), and adults are often available from pet stores that sell reptiles. Allow mice to warm to room temperature before introducing them into a cage. To speed thawing, soak the mice in warm water or place them a few inches from an incandescent light, but don't get them so hot that they cook. Do *not* put frozen mice in the microwave to thaw them out. What often happens in this case is that the mice will explode.

Feed hatchling and subadult kingsnakes one or two mice every two to seven days, depending on your desired rate of growth. As a rule, snakes will grow faster if offered small food items two or more times a week, rather than a single large food item once a week. First, smaller food items are easier to digest. Second, over a given period of time, snakes fed smaller food items every two to three days will be able to consume a greater amount of food. The feeding schedule can be reduced in the winter months, although until kingsnakes reach breeding size, most herpetoculturists aim for a rapid and steady growth rate. It is not uncommon, however, for juvenile kingsnakes to spontaneously go off feed for varying periods of time during the winter months. To continue obtaining a good growth rate, make sure that you keep the temperature gradients within the recommended range, which is 77°F–86°F (25°C–30°C) for maintenance, and offer food frequently. A snake that refuses food on a given day may decide to feed the next day.

Within any given clutch, there usually will be one or more stubborn or picky feeders. Before trying alternative methods, you should explore all the variations of offering pinky mice: live, prekilled, prekilled and washed to remove scent, and prekilled with brain matter smeared on the prey's head and anterior parts of its body. The latter method sounds gruesome, but we are talking about a dead mouse and, surprisingly often, the method works.

Scenting

If the above methods fail, try the scenting method, a well-proven trick to get reluctant kingsnake hatchlings started on pinkies: rinse a prekilled mouse in water, dry it off, and then rub it against the skin of a lizard. (Some keepers get dead anoles or skinks from a pet shop and keep them in the freezer for such uses.)

Other scenting methods include offering a prekilled pinky with its mouth stuffed with a piece of lizard tail and sticking a piece of feeder lizard on the head of the prekilled mouse. Fence lizards (*Sceloporus* spp.) are ideal animals to use as they are natural food for many kingsnakes. However, most commonly available lizards, including green anoles, will provide the scent necessary to trigger a feeding response.

If the snake still refuses to feed on pinkies, you may try offering your stubborn snake a feeder lizard. Most pet stores will sell an inexpensive lizard that should work. The key here is to obtain the smallest animal possible, one that can be easily swallowed. Slightly raising the ambient air temperature in which the snake is kept (by 3-5 degrees Fahrenheit [1-2 degrees Celsius]) may also stimulate a feeding response. If for some reason nothing seems to work, then force-feeding is the last resort.

Force-Feeding

To force-feed a hatchling, gently hold the snake behind its head with your thumb and forefinger while holding the rest of its body down on a solid, stable surface. Ideally, a prekilled newborn mouse should be used (the smaller the better). If you cannot obtain a day-old mouse or if a snake is unusually small, then a section of leg or section of tail from a weaned, prekilled mouse can be used. (If a mouse leg is used, make sure there are no bones sticking out through the skin or where it was separated from the body.) With your free hand holding round-tipped forceps, grab the pinky or mouse leg, lubricate it with water, and insert it headfirst or thigh end-first into the snake's mouth.

The least stressful part to force-feed to a snake is a mouse tail. Insert the tail thick end-first so the bristly hairs

As your snake grows, you can increase the prey size from pinkies to just-weaned mice such as the one this California kingsnake is devouring.

lie flat as the tail is inserted. Often, if the section of leg or tail is inserted just past the throat, and the snake is immediately placed back into its cage and left undisturbed, it will proceed to swallow the section on its own.

If the snake regurgitates, you may have to repeat the procedure, gently pushing the section well past the throat area into the body. (*Caution*: This can be dangerous if you are not experienced; seek the help of a knowledgeable keeper.) Most reluctant common kingsnake feeders will begin to feed on their own after two or three force-feedings.

Feeding Subadults

As a kingsnake grows, the size of the prey will have to increase accordingly. A good general rule is for the prey item to have a girth equal to or up to one and one-quarter times the apparent girth of the snake. Thus, hatchlings will graduate from hairless pinky mice to fuzzy mice to just-weaned mice (sometimes called hoppers) and so on. As with hatchlings, one to two mice per feeding should be adequate. Until kingsnakes reach breeding size (usually after two years), they should continue to be fed every two to seven days. The growth rate should be rapid up to two or three years and will begin to taper off after breeding size is reached.

Feeding Adults

Adult kingsnakes should be fed adult mice or just-weaned rats (for larger snakes) on a regimen that will be determined by their breeding schedule (see chapter 7). If you're not interested in breeding but only in keeping kingsnakes as pets, a feeding schedule of one to three adult mice per week per adult snake is adequate. The number of mice used will have to be determined in part by the appearance of the snake and by its size. A large eastern kingsnake or Florida kingsnake will become quite lean on a diet of just one mouse per week. You will have to adjust the diet so the snake maintains a smooth, rounded body without the outline of the ribs or backbone being prominent. As a general rule, kingsnakes 4 feet (1.2 m) or more will require at least two adult mice a week to maintain good weight.

Feeding Regimen for Breeding Kingsnakes

For those of you who hibernate your kingsnakes to condition them for breeding, you will have to stop all feeding ten to fifteen days prior to cooling. This is a necessary precaution to allow the snakes to empty their digestive systems. Most herpetoculturists prepare their kingsnakes for breeding sometime in November or December, partially depending on when temperatures drop enough to allow cooling of a hibernation room where snakes are maintained.

Upon return to normal temperatures following a cooling period (usually in March), kingsnakes can be returned to a normal feeding schedule. Herpetoculturists usually wait a few days to a week before beginning to offer food. With most subspecies (speckled kings, which breed early, are an exception), there is an interval of a few weeks during which kingsnakes will readily feed before they actually begin breeding. The first or second shed of the female after removal from hibernation is often associated with the actual onset of the breeding period. If a snake is a little thin following removal from hibernation, it is important that you feed more frequent, somewhat smaller meals during

Hibernation Versus Brumation

It is important to recognize that snakes do not hibernate during the winter months in the literal sense of the word. *Hibernation* implies a state of dormancy wherein an animal is inactive. The scant research that has been done on reptile behavior suggests that the animals will emerge from their winter shelters during days that are abnormally warm. This type of wintering behavior, in which there may be continual albeit reduced activity, is called *brumation*. Most herpetoculturists, however, continue to refer to the cooling process and the reduced activity associated with it as "hibernation." Because the meaning of hibernation in a herpetocultural sense is generally understood, the author will continue to use *hibernation* and *hibernate* in the rest of the text.

this prebreeding window to allow the snake to reach an adequate weight. This can be critical to your breeding success.

During breeding season, males often will be so frenzied that they may not feed readily (they have their priorities). Following copulations and as gestation progresses, female kingsnakes typically feed less frequently and sometimes go off feed altogether. The key to continuous feeding of females is to offer smaller prey more often. One of the reasons female snakes feed less frequently when gravid appears to be linked to the fact that developing eggs take up increasingly more room in the abdominal cavity. Large food items, which create large lumps and large fecal masses, often will be refused during this time, whereas smaller food items will be accepted. Gravid female kingsnakes that are going off feed should be frequently offered one or two fuzzy mice, small fuzzy rats, or large pinky rats. Do not offer inordinately large numbers of food items; if you do, you will cause the female to regurgitate. Offering a small number of smaller-than-normal food items often (every two to three days) is the right course of action. It is important to keep gravid females on an optimal feeding regimen during the breeding period, not only to prevent any significant depletion of body weight but also to help stimulate egg production for another clutch. According to Robert Applegate, a well-known and successful colubrid breeder, feedings during this time can make the difference between a single clutch and a second clutch of eggs.

Male kingsnakes usually need little or no inducement to feed except when in shed, although many males stop feeding when in close proximity to females during the breeding season. If this happens, try putting the male in a separate room until he starts feeding again. The feeding schedule for males should be similar to that of females during the breeding season. Watch that your male does not become overweight. If this happens, gradually reduce the meals to one or two food items per meal.

A feeding schedule of two to four adult mice should be initiated for a female immediately after she has deposited her eggs. (See chapter 7 for additional information on feeding regimens for breeding kingsnakes.)

CHAPTER 6

Diseases and Disorders

Both wild-caught and captive-bred kingsnakes can exhibit a number of diseases and disorders. These often are the result of environmental stress, improper maintenance, or the introduction of new animals into an established collection. Careful attention to vivarium design, temperature, and husbandry procedures is important to minimize stress. Any new animals should be quarantined for a minimum of four weeks, checked for parasites (internal and external), and treated accordingly before being introduced into a collection. Following are some of the more common problems of kingsnakes and recommended treatments for those problems.

External Parasites

Two types of external parasites snake keepers have to deal with are ticks and mites. Wild-caught animals sometimes have ticks imbedded in their skin; ticks should be removed carefully and immediately. For any reptile keeper, mites are a scourge. Once introduced, they are very difficult to get rid of, so it is extremely important to immediately treat infected snakes, preferably in quarantine.

Ticks

To remove a tick, use a cotton swab to apply a drop or two of rubbing alcohol to its body. After five minutes, you can easily remove the tick with tweezers. If there are several ticks to be removed, then apply a pyrethrin-based spray to a cloth and wipe the snake with it. Later, the dead ticks will drop off or can be easily removed.

When using products with pyrethrin, rinse the animal in lukewarm water after treatment. It has been suggested that when pyrethrins are misused, they can cause respiratory problems and damage the lenses of the eyes. Although pyrethrins are usually safe, some keepers suggest that hatchlings not be treated with commercial miticides. It is a good idea to consult your veterinarian before proceeding.

There are different concentrations of pyrethrins. Restrict usage to those products with a concentration of less than 0.3 percent. *Warning*: Be aware that you can absorb pyrethrins through your skin. Always wear gloves, a face mask, and eye protection when using these sprays.

Mites

Mites usually can be seen as tiny, dark, blood-filled, beadlike creatures moving about on the surface of a snake. Sometimes very tiny mites (ones that are young) appear much lighter. They are easier to spot when the snake is about to shed, as this displaces them temporarily. A good indicator of mites is the presence of silvery white specks on the skin of a snake. These specks are mite feces and will cause a snake to appear covered with white dust when large numbers of mites are present.

Pyrethrin sprays are very effective in eliminating mites. (See paragraph above on the proper pyrethrin sprays to use and what protective clothing to wear when using.) Cages and cage contents can also be treated with pyrethrins. It is best to use a cloth dampened with the spray and wiped on the skin of the snake. Leave the pyrethrin on the animal for ten to twenty minutes before rinsing it off. Repeat the treatment in two to three weeks.

Warning: Be very careful when using miticides on hatchlings; because of their small size, they are more vulnerable to respiratory problems, damage to the eye lenses, or death caused by the miticide.

Snakes infested with mites should be seen by a veterinarian. Mites are blood suckers and can cause life-threatening anemias; they also carry deadly diseases.

Don't Forget the Cage!

Don't forget that a mite infestation occurs not only on the snake but also on the cage's contents and on both the inside and outside surfaces of the cage. The entire cage and all of its contents need to be disinfected with household bleach and thoroughly rinsed. Cage contents that cannot be disinfected should be thrown out and replaced. You should also wipe the surrounding area with pyrethrins or at least a bleach solution. (Always wear gloves, a face mask, and eye protection when using these chemicals.) Mites often come back after treatment because most products do not kill the mite eggs that lie at the bottom of a cage or on cage furniture. To successfully treat mites in a collection, you must also treat and disinfect the enclosure. Obviously, these parasites are a major headache and should be prevented from being introduced into a collection. Thoroughly inspecting a snake prior to purchase and quarantining newly purchased snakes for a minimum of four weeks are highly recommended procedures.

A somewhat controversial method for mite treatment that many people have nevertheless found to be effective is the use of No-Pest Strips soaked with dichlorvos (2,2-dichlorovinyl dimethyl phosphate). A strip 1 inch wide × 2 inches long (2.5 cm × 5 cm) is enough to kill mites on kingsnakes in most enclosures. The strip should be put in some sort of perforated container so there is *no direct contact* with the snake. Depending on the type of cage that you keep your snake in, air circulation should be kept to a minimum during treatment, which should last between twelve hours and twenty-four hours.

Warning: Remember, however, that this treatment is controversial. Damage to internal organs of vertebrates, especially the liver, has been linked to overexposure to these chemicals. Consult with a veterinarian before proceeding.

Any reptile veterinarian should have access to products for mite treatment that are relatively safe and effective, especially ones for long-term usage. One of these is an ivermectin solution in spray form for topical applications. Safe miticides are widely available in pet shops, but be sure to precisely follow all instructions.

Another safe method for killing mites is to sprinkle carbaryl (Sevin) dust (available in nurseries and supermarkets) on newspaper at the bottom of a cage. This powder will kill mites within twenty-four hours. The treatment should be repeated in about ten days.

Internal Parasites

Ideally, fresh stool samples from all wild-collected kingsnakes should be analyzed by a veterinarian to determine whether the snakes have internal parasites. This is a relatively simple and inexpensive procedure in most cases, but get an estimate beforehand. A veterinarian will be able to prescribe an effective treatment protocol if there is a problem. The following are some internal parasites a kingsnake may have and need treatment for:

- Nematodes (roundworms, including lungworms)
- Cestodes (tapeworms)
- Pentastomes (tongue worms, which infest the respiratory tract)
- Protozoans (such as *Entamoeba* sp., *Giardia* sp., and *Trichomonas* sp.)

Infectious Stomatitis (Mouth Rot)

Although stomatitis (mouth rot) is not common in kingsnakes, neither wild-caught nor captive-bred, it does occasionally turn up in specimens kept in collections over time. Mouth injuries often predispose a snake to mouth rot. Watch for the early warning signs in snakes with injured mouths. Mouth rot, which attacks the tissue of the gums, can be caused by bacterial infections, viruses, and fungi, as well as various metabolic problems and cancer. Symptoms

By carefully opening your kingsnake's mouth, you can check for cuts or sores. The presence of cheeselike matter is evidence of infectious stomatitis (mouth rot), a serious disease requiring immediate treatment.

vary depending upon the severity of the condition. Swelling along the jawline and reluctance to feed are early symptoms noticed by most snake keepers. If a snake has mouth rot, it will have an accumulation of caseous matter along the gumline. Infectious stomatitis is a very serious disease. Although some publications on snake keeping offer advice on how to treat your snake yourself, the wiser and safer course is to consult your veterinarian immediately. Any delay in treatment could lead to the death of your snake.

Skin Disorders

The most common skin disorder involves the inability of the snake to shed its skin, whether in one piece or in several pieces. As most snake keepers know, a healthy snake usually sheds its skin in one piece. A problem shed will be characterized by shed skin, including eye caps (spectacles), remaining attached to the body. The most common cause of a problem shed is improper husbandry, which includes improper ambient temperatures or ambient humidity or the lack of proper cage furniture (such as a water bowl large enough for the snake to soak in). Certain diseases, such as skin infections or mite infestations, can also cause shedding problems.

Skin blisters are another skin disorder. They look like little white bumps under the scales and cause the scales to rise.

Shedding Problems

Usually, a snake will shed within the first week after the clearing of preshedding conditions (eyes with a milky blue and clouded appearance; skin dull, opaque, and dry looking). If the snake fails to shed within this period, you should consider soaking it to soften its old skin and facilitate shedding. The usual course of treatment when a snake has a problem shed is to place the snake in a plastic storage box (with holes for aeration) in which a small amount of water, equal to approximately half the thickness of the snake's body, has been placed. The lid is replaced and secured with strong tape, unless you are using a rack system in which the shelving is flush with the top of the box. The snake is then allowed to soak for approximately twelve hours. The remaining shed may have come off by then as a result of the activity of the snake. If not, the shed skin will be easily removed by hand by

A healthy snake, such as the Florida kingsnake shown here, sheds its skin in one piece.

This eastern king is in midshed. Healthy snakes typically have no problem shedding their skins, but incorrect enclosure temperature or humidity levels may affect your healthy pet's ability to shed properly.

gently pulling or slipping it off. There are also products now available in pet stores that aid in the removal of old skin from snakes. Talk to your veterinarian about what products to use.

A simple way to remove a retained spectacle (eye cap) is to place a piece of cellophane tape over the eye cap, then gently pull the tape off. If there is a retained eye cap, it will usually come off with the tape. *Note*: If you don't see a cap come off with the tape, wait until the next shed, then reevaluate the need for a visit to your veterinarian.

Removing old eye caps requires a delicate touch, and caution is advised so that no damage is done to the cornea, which can lead to blindness . If there is any doubt as to whether an eye cap is still present (sometimes it is difficult to tell), consult your veterinarian.

Skin Blister Disease

Normally, the associated cause for skin blisters is a cage that is kept too wet or one that combines old feces and a wet substrate. Either way, poor maintenance practices allow bacteria that produce the problem to grow. Skin blisters can also be caused by fungi.

The initial treatment is to put the snake in a clean, dry cage on clean substrate and provide water in a small dish that does not allow for soaking. Wipe the snake with a warm, wet cloth to remove any dirt or foreign substance. Then consult your veterinarian about further treatment.

Note: Some sources recommend that you apply a topical povidone-iodine solution to the skin with a cloth once a day, and consult a veterinarian only if the disease appears extensive. However, skin blisters are a sign of serious systemic disease. Animals with any evidence of skin disease should be taken to a veterinarian for proper treatment.

Rodent Bites

There is no reason for rodent bites to occur because kingsnakes readily accept prekilled rodents. Feeding prekilled prey is not only more humane to the prey but also safer for the snake. A live mouse or rat left overnight (or sometimes even for a few hours without supervision) with a snake is very likely to inflict deep bites on the snake.

If your snake has been bitten by a rodent, you can begin treatment by cleansing the area with povidone-iodine solution, removing any loose skin or tissue, and applying a topical antibacterial ointment. You should then seek treatment from your veterinarian. He or she can administer pain medication and, if the wound has become infected, an injectable antibiotic.

Respiratory Infections

There are many causes of respiratory infections in snakes. Improper husbandry, poor nutrition, and stress are at the root of most cases. Respiratory infections may occur in kingsnakes that are kept at constant intermediate temperatures, too cool for normal activity and effective digestion and too warm to induce the state of metabolic rest usually associated with hibernation. Other factors, including an overall poor state of health, will increase susceptibility to respiratory infections.

In the earliest stage of a respiratory infection, the symptoms are usually decreased activity, reluctance to feed, and the presence of increased bubbly mucus inside the mouth. As the disease progresses into pneumonia, the amount of mucus increases, sometimes emerging through the sides of the mouth. The snake will gape as it struggles to breathe and will exhale forcibly. In the early stages, maintaining the snake at uniformly higher temperatures of 86°F–90°F (30°C–32°C) around the clock usually will help a snake's immune system fight off the infection, but seek veterinary help right away. Do not wait until the snake's condition deteriorates; by then, it may be too late.

There are other causes of respiratory diseases. In wild-collected kingsnakes, high parasite loads (lungworms in particular) can cause respiratory distress, which results in gaping.

Reactions to chemical irritants are another cause—for example, to the substrate and, more commonly, ammonia gas released by accumulating feces in an enclosure that is too wet. Many a herpetoculturist upon opening a fouled cage has been struck by the strong ammonia smell. Long-term exposure to this gas can affect a snake's respiratory system.

Gastrointestinal Infections

Any kingsnake that refuses food or regularly regurgitates food and also has diarrhea or discolored, unusually smelly, or bloody stools should be taken to a veterinarian to determine the cause. Untreated snakes with these symptoms usually die. With proper diagnosis and treatment, however, the prognosis for a cure and long-term survival is usually good.

Quarantine any snake with the above symptoms, and adopt strict procedures to make sure that you don't infect other animals in your collection.

- Do not use any tools used for the maintenance of the infected snake on other snakes; disinfect these tools in a bleach solution (such as sodium hypochlorite) after use.
- Perform maintenance of any sick snakes *after* handling the healthy snakes in your collection.
- Thoroughly wash your hands with a disinfectant following any maintenance or handling of the infected snake. In fact, do so after handling any snake.

Visual Assessment of Health

Routine visual inspection of your snake should be an integral part of your husbandry techniques. Inspections should be made on a daily basis to help prevent serious ailments.

- **Muscle tone and vigor:** Does the snake move about the cage in an easy manner? Are there any depressed areas on the body? When the snake is picked up, does it feel strong and vigorous in its movements, or does it feel relatively sluggish?
- **Weight:** Can you see the backbone or ribs through the skin even though the snake eats well?
- **Eyes, mouth, and vent:** Do the eyes appear to be clear and alert without being sunken in? Are there any lumps, bumps, or bruises on or around the mouth? Is the vent area clean and free of any caked or runny fecal matter?
- **Fecal assessment:** Do the feces appear firm with proper color, or are they watery, off-color, or terribly foul smelling?
- **Behavior:** Is the snake gaping its mouth? Does it appear to have a loss of equilibrium or to be listless?

If you notice any of the above problems, you should visit the veterinarian, consult reference manuals, or discuss the situation with other herpetoculturists to assess the possible cause of the problem. Runny stools, blood in the stools, or unusual weight loss should almost always be investigated through a fecal analysis—a procedure best performed by a qualified veterinarian. Visually checking your snake's cage daily will also help eliminate potential health risks. Make sure substrate material is clean and dry, cage furniture is secure, and water and water bowls are clean. Any shed skin should be removed along with any fecal matter.

You should establish a relationship with a qualified reptile veterinarian. That way, when a problem arises, you have someone you can turn to for help. Keep your veterinarian's contact information handy so anyone watching your collection can contact the doctor in an emergency.

CHAPTER 7

Breeding

Kingsnakes are *oviparous*, meaning that they lay eggs that develop and hatch outside the female's body. In the wild, common kingsnakes breed between March and June. Captive kingsnakes, with proper conditioning, will breed during the same months that wild kingsnakes do, although some breeders manipulate the cooling cycle so that breeding is spread out over a greater period of time. Common kingsnakes in captivity will typically breed within a few weeks following their removal from hibernation and return to a normal maintenance schedule. The first or second shed by a female following her removal from hibernation is associated with sexual readiness and the production of pheromones that play a key role in successful copulation. A female kingsnake usually will lay eggs four to eight weeks following copulation, although that time interval could extend to as much as twelve weeks.

Biting is a common courtship practice.

The clutch sizes of common kingsnakes range anywhere from three to twenty-four eggs, with the average number of eggs per clutch in the low to middle teens. The size of a female and her age, health, and genetic factors will play key roles in the number of eggs she may produce. Many common kingsnakes, if large and provided with enough food, will lay two clutches of eggs during the breeding season.

The incubation of kingsnake eggs usually lasts from six to ten weeks, possibly longer, depending on incubation temperature. Newly hatched kingsnakes are from 8-13 inches (20-33 cm) long and usually shed within the first week.

Before Breeding Kingsnakes

There are certain considerations you need to address before you attempt to breed kingsnakes. First, of course, you must be certain you have at least one male and one female. If you're uncertain about the sex of your animals, have them sexed by an experienced herpetoculturist.

The next consideration is the age of your snakes. Successful breeding can occur only with sexually mature animals. Most captive-bred kingsnakes must be at least two years old to successfully breed. Size is a good criterion for determining sexual maturity. Most sexually mature common kingsnakes are at least 36 inches (91 cm) long; although kingsnakes may breed at a smaller size, 36 inches is the minimum size used by most breeders. Another criterion for determining maturity is age. The rule of thumb for kingsnakes used to be eighteen months until sexual maturity if a snake had been maintained on an optimal growth feeding schedule. Many breeders prefer to wait an additional year to allow for extra growth.

Breeding at minimal size or an early age can result in stunting that will ultimately affect the breeding ability of a snake. This also increases chances for a snake to become egg-bound, which occurs when the female is unable to lay her eggs because they have extremely thin shells or perhaps no shells at all. Egg-binding is uncomfortable for snakes and, in extreme cases, can lead to death. In order to avoid egg-binding, many breeders choose to wait until their snakes are at least two years old (usually two and a half) before attempting to breed them.

The other important consideration before conditioning your kingsnakes for breeding is the status of their health. A snake that is not in prime condition should never be considered for breeding. Not only will the chances for successful breeding diminish but the actual gestation period may be life threatening as well. The chances of the female's becoming egg-bound also significantly increase if she is ill, underweight, or undersize.

Steps to Successful Breeding

Although there are many subspecies of kingsnakes inhabiting diverse terrains, altitudes, and climatic zones, general parameters for successful breeding can be applied to all subspecies. These parameters include prebreeding conditioning that may involve cooling, proper feeding regimens, introducing snakes for breeding, monitoring the females, providing egg-laying sites, and ensuring proper egg incubation.

Prebreeding Conditioning

The standard procedure for prebreeding conditioning of kingsnakes involves cooling them for at least two months at a specific, constant, lowered temperature range. All the subspecies of kingsnakes may be conditioned for breeding by using this procedure. Because of the possibility of activity during hibernation, always provide fresh water in topple-proof containers during the cooling period. Fill the containers halfway to eliminate possible water spillage.

As a general rule, kingsnakes should be cooled to between 50°F and 60°F (10°C and 16°C) for a period of eight to twelve weeks. Most kingsnakes, however, will safely tolerate temperature drops into the upper 40s F (7°-9°C). During this cooling period, lights should be turned off or the photoperiod (the ratio of daylight to darkness provided) significantly reduced. Some kingsnake breeders pay careful attention to the photoperiod during this time and suggest that it is at least as important as cooling. Other successful breeders simply keep their snakes in dark areas during the entire cooling period. Basically, the photoperiod is reduced to ten hours or less for the winter months.

During hibernation, it is important to regularly check snakes for any signs of diseases, especially respiratory infections. Skin blisters are commonly caused by soggy substrates. If there is a problem, the snake should be removed from hibernation immediately and treated accordingly. The probability of any illnesses happening is significantly reduced if the snake is in top condition prior to the cooling period. If you have any doubts about a snake's health, do not hibernate it.

These prebreeding procedures are necessary for consistent breeding success and high fertility rates. The dormant period in cool conditions is believed to cause female kingsnakes to produce hormones that stimulate ovulation and pheromones (sex hormones) that elicit sexual behavior in males. The cooling period triggers an increase in hormone levels in males, too, which elicits mating behavior and the production of healthy, active sperm.

Feeding Regimen

When you first remove kingsnakes from cooling, check their health immediately. Prompt attention to any health problems may allow an affected snake (or snakes) to still be bred. If the snakes are healthy coming out of hibernation, then conditioning for breeding can commence right away. Warming the animals to normal maintenance temperatures and providing an extended photoperiod are the first steps. Many commercial breeders, however, pay no attention to the photoperiod, as kingsnakes will breed in low-light conditions.

The snakes should be tried on food within two to three days after their return to normal maintenance temperatures. Be aware, however, that it can sometimes take a week to ten days out of hibernation before kingsnakes start feeding.

When kingsnakes start feeding after hibernation, they usually do so with gusto. As during normal maintenance procedures, snakes should always be separated during feeding. From the time that kingsnakes are taken out of hibernation

Here, a male California king has inserted his hemipenis into a female's cloaca. Copulation usually occurs immediately after introduction; the male holds the female with his mouth and positions his body so the snakes are vent to vent.

until the sexual pairs are introduced for breeding, the feeding period can be critical—especially for somewhat underweight specimens. In females, intensive feeding during this period can play a crucial role in their fecundity for a given year.

Right after hibernation, start by giving one or two rodents of appropriate size to each snake every two to three days. Two to four large mice or fuzzy rats can be fed to very large specimens, such as *L. g. getula*, every two or three days. Kingsnakes usually are able to handle this amount of food. Some might want more, some less, or they might not want to eat quite that often. In any event, the feeding pattern should be established within the first week and adhered to throughout this phase of conditioning. A snake that is reluctant to start feeding might be offered a smaller-than-normal rodent. Offer food frequently until the snake starts feeding readily.

The length of time this accelerated feeding schedule lasts is determined to a significant degree by how soon the snake is ready to breed. A primary purpose of accelerated feeding is to put weight on snakes that are slightly under-weight after removal from hibernation. Usually, a three- to six-week period is sufficient to prime both sexes for breeding. Because snakes lose very little weight during hibernation, a snake coming out of hibernation thin prob-ably went into hibernation being thin. A snake that is obvi-ously underweight should not be hibernated.

The Breeding Window

There is a critical breeding window, the onset of which is usually associated with the first shed following removal from hibernation. Waiting too long may cause the snakes to be out of breeding synchronization, which could result in little or no breeding success.

After a female kingsnake is removed from hibernation, her first shed (possibly second shed if she is already under-going a shed cycle upon removal from hibernation) is usu-ally associated with ovulation and the production of phero-mones. In general, you should begin introduction of pairs following the first post-hibernation shed. Many breeders start introductions earlier. In the case of speckled king-snakes, which breed soon after removal from hibernation, pairs are introduced for short periods of time starting one week after their return to normal maintenance schedules.

One way to be certain a female is ready to breed is to feel for developing ovarian egg follicles. This procedure is re-ferred to as palpation. Palpating a female kingsnake involves gently pushing in the ventral scales toward the backbone, starting at about midbody and continuing toward the vent. The follicles feel like a series of bumps. If you can feel the follicles, then your snake is ready to breed, and a male should be introduced. Gentle palpation is the key to determining if follicles have formed; you can even determine the number of eggs that will be laid.

Copulation usually occurs immediately following introduction, with the male chasing the female around the cage until she is caught. The male normally grabs the female with his mouth, holds her behind the head, and positions his body so their vents meet; one of the male's hemipenes enters the female's cloaca, and copulation occurs. This will last anywhere from several minutes to several hours. If successive breedings occur, the male will alternate hemipenes each time.

The snakes can be kept together for two to three days, until they must be fed. Then they should be separated so they can feed safely, and the male has time to regenerate sperm for the next breeding. They should be reintroduced several times over the next three to four weeks to ensure high fertility.

If there are several pairs involved, then it may be wise to introduce the females to more than one male unless you are involved in careful line-breeding, which requires that exact records are maintained as to the father of a particular group of offspring. If careful line-breeding is not a factor, then using more than one male is a wise precaution in case one of the males is infertile. Even if you're not line-breeding,

Note the harmless stains on the shells of these eggs, which are resting on sphagnum moss.

keeping careful breeding records will allow you to determine which males tend to perform consistently. A "dud" male may copulate without releasing viable sperm because of one or more factors that have led to sterility. Any successful breeding program should involve more than one pair of snakes to minimize the possibility of relying on a sterile male. A useful method for determining the fertility of males and probable successful copulation is to obtain a cloacal smear from a recently copulated female. The smear can then be examined under a microscope at a low magnification to check for the presence of active sperm.

Gestation

After you are certain that the snakes have bred, separate the females from the males. A gravid female snake demonstrates significant abdominal swelling that usually can be seen easily or can be palpated readily even when the eggs are still small. In most cases, a gravid female also becomes reluctant to feed on large prey and may go off feed completely as gestation progresses. A good indication that the female is about to lay eggs is the pre-egg-laying shed (usually the second shed after removal from hibernation). This normally occurs five to ten days before the eggs are laid.

Feeding schedules, as discussed earlier, should be followed, and a nest box should be put into the female's cage. This box should be large enough so the snake can get in and lay her eggs. I have used a 2-quart (1.9-L) plastic storage container with moistened vermiculite; the container has a small hole cut in the lid to allow for entry. The timing of putting the nest box in the cage is a matter of choice, although it should be done no later than the pre-egg-laying shed. The time between copulation and egg deposition in kingsnakes usually ranges from six to twelve weeks.

As noted, a female kingsnake may go off feed or refuse larger prey as gestation progresses. This should not be a problem if a female has good weight. Offer gravid females small prey animals, such as fuzzy mice, if they refuse larger adult mice.

Incubation

Once the eggs have been deposited—in the nest box, one hopes—they should be set up in an appropriate incubator. The system does not need to be too complex, as the eggs just have to be kept at the same temperature as your snakes but with higher humidity. This can be accomplished by burying the eggs halfway in moist vermiculite (equal parts of vermiculite and water by weight) contained in a plastic storage box with a few small holes for air exchange, which is very important for developing embryos.

Most of the time, eggs are deposited in a clump with the shells adhering to each other. Do not separate the eggs; you may damage them. I have successfully hatched many clutches of eggs that were clumped together. Sometimes one or more infertile eggs may be included in a clump of good eggs. The bad eggs will become obvious after a few weeks of incubation. Don't try to remove them from the rest. I have also successfully hatched many clutches of eggs in this condition.

Eggs should be incubated at a constant temperature of 82°F–84°F (28°C–29°C) in a coarse grade of vermiculite that has been mixed with an equal amount of water by weight. The vermiculite should feel barely moist and not waterlogged. An

Two babies from this Florida kingsnake clutch slither away from the nest site as two others finally break through their shells.

easy method of incubation is to use an aquarium with a few inches of water on the bottom, heated by a submersible aquarium heater. The temperature should be adjusted with the aid of a thermometer, allowing several days of lead time before eggs are introduced. As stated earlier, a plastic storage box is suitable for incubating eggs. The box, with moistened vermiculite, is placed on bricks or a sturdy wire rack above the water and allowed to heat up to the ambient air temperature within the aquarium. The humidity is regulated by partially covering the top of the aquarium. The eggs should be placed in the incubator when the temperature of the vermiculite in the incubator box has stabilized to 82°F–84°F (28°C–29°C) for at least forty-eight hours.

The babies should hatch in eight to ten weeks. Like most snakes, kingsnakes will not emerge immediately after slitting their shells. It is *very* important not to attempt to help them hatch because their lungs may not be fully developed yet. Only twenty-four hours after the snake has first poked its head out should you consider providing help.

There are occasions when the baby will shred the shell with its egg tooth and become stuck between shell sections. When this happens, use cuticle scissors to make 90-degree

This group of hatchling albino California kingsnakes soon will need to be separated. Problems with cannibalism are more common among hatchling and subadult kings.

A hatchling Florida king checks out its new surroundings. House your hatchlings separately to allow monitoring of activities such as their first sheds and feeding regularity.

incisions through the slits in the shell sections made by the hatching snake. Snakes that have failed to slit their shells within thirty-six hours of the rest of the clutch should be assisted by making a 1 inch x ¼ inch (25 mm x 6 mm) incision at the high point of the top side of the egg. These incisions are made so that only the shell is pierced; the scissors *must not* penetrate any deeper.

Hatchling kingsnakes need to be maintained separately in individual enclosures. This will allow for close monitoring of each animal and will allow you to determine when a snake first sheds, how well it feeds, and whether it needs any special attention. Caging animals individually also will prevent the possibility of cannibalism occurring during feeding. Refer to chapter 5, if necessary.

Double-Clutching

There are several factors that can influence the production of a second clutch of eggs.

- **Age and size:** It is best to attempt double-clutching with older, larger females.

- **Health and relative weight:** It is important to observe the condition of the female after she lays her first clutch. She must be in good health, not too thin or lethargic.
- **Timing of the introduction of a male followed by an appropriate feeding regimen:** If the female appears relatively robust, then proceed to introduce her to a male soon after she has laid her eggs. Don't assume copulation will occur because timing is everything. It has been reported that if this second introduction occurs too late in the year, the female won't be interested in breeding. If copulation is observed, then you must assume she has been impregnated and proceed with an accelerated feeding schedule once again.
- **Accelerated feeding schedule:** This involves feeding two or three adult mice or fuzzy rats every three to four days. Again, it is probable that the female will become a reluctant feeder during gestation and should be offered small food items to try to get her to feed. For double-clutching, proper feeding during the first clutching is essential.

Notes on Breeding Various Subspecies

Blotched Kingsnakes and South Florida Kingsnakes (*L. g. "goini"* and *"brooksi"*)

- **Minimum breeding age:** Two to three years.
- **When cooled:** Start cooling in December to the beginning of March. However, these subspecies can be cooled for only two months with good breeding success.
- **Temperature for cooling:** In the mid-50s F (13°C).
- **Pairing:** Sexual pairs are introduced mid-March, although the vast majority of breeding takes place in April.
- **When eggs are laid:** Six to eight weeks after breeding. Most eggs are laid in June, although females can lay first clutches as early as May.
- **Clutch size:** Ten to twenty eggs are laid per clutch, with sixteen to seventeen on average.

- **Number of clutches:** Both subspecies will double-clutch if properly maintained and conditioned for breeding, especially *L. g. "goini."*
- **Breeding difficulties:** None.

California, Desert, Mexican Black, and Yuma Kingsnakes (*L. g. californiae, splendida, nigrita,* and *"yumensis"*)

- **Minimum breeding age:** Two to three years.
- **When cooled:** December to March.
- **Temperature for cooling:** In the low to mid-50s F (10°C–12°C).
- **Pairing:** All four forms breed six weeks after hibernation.
- **When eggs are laid:** Six to eight weeks after breeding.
- **Clutch size:** California king—six to twenty-three for coastal types, six to twelve for desert phase; desert king—six to twelve; Mexican black king—six to twenty; Yuma king—six to twelve.
- **Number of clutches:** These subspecies commonly will double-clutch if healthy and well fed.
- **Breeding difficulties:** These are easy breeders with few problems.

Speckled Kingsnakes (*L. g. holbrooki*)

- **Minimum breeding age:** Two to three years.
- **When cooled:** December to March.
- **Temperature for cooling:** In the low to mid-50s F (10°C–12°C).
- **Pairing:** This subspecies is atypical in that pairs must be introduced no later than two weeks after removal from hibernation; they will breed as early as one week after.
- **When eggs are laid:** Six to eight weeks after breeding.
- **Clutch size:** Six to twenty-two eggs.
- **Number of clutches:** Will double-clutch if female is large. Smaller females don't double-clutch.
- **Breeding difficulties:** None, except for early introduction of pairs.

CHAPTER 8

Subspecies of the Common Kingsnake

Following are the seven recognized (by herpetologists) and six unrecognized (except by herpetoculturists) subspecies of the common kingsnake.

Detailed analysis of the molecular genetics of these snakes now shows with some certainty that five full species can be recognized: *L. getula* (including *floridana*); *L. nigra*; *L. holbrooki*; *L. splendida* (including *nigrita*); and *L. californiae*. Expect to see this usage of the scientific names become more common in the years ahead.

Recognized Subspecies

Numbered among the recognized subspecies are the highly variable **California kingsnake**, which comes in several colors and forms; the **Florida kingsnake**, generally brown with yellowish coloring on each scale; the **eastern kingsnake**, alternatively called the chain kingsnake because of the distinct pattern of connected, light-colored crossbands extending across the back; the **speckled kingsnake**, so named for the cream to yellow spot on each of the dark brown or black scales that cover the entire back; the **black snake**, which despite its name, does have some light spots; the **Mexican black kingsnake**, which in its pure form is usually all black or very dark brown; and the **desert kingsnake**, which has dark brown to black background color with numerous yellow or white spots on the sides.

California Kingsnake (*L. g. californiae*)

The California kingsnake ranges from the southern tip of the Baja Peninsula in Mexico up to southern Oregon and from the western coast of California across to the desert areas of

For California kings, herpetoculturists emphasize either a sharply contrasted pattern as seen in banded morphs or, as shown with this high-yellow morph, nearly absent markings.

Nevada and Arizona. The geographic variants established in herpetoculture include pattern and color morphs.

The most widely recognized pattern morphs are: striped, banded, aberrant (variable but sometimes consistent pattern variations that don't fit the striped, banded, or other pattern categories), patternless (chocolate), Newport-Long Beach (patterns characterized by the relative width of light banding or a high percentage of light coloration and reduction of dark col-

The banana king shown here is a reverse of the chocolate morph, which is mostly brown with yellow bands.

oration), and the patternless albino (snow king). Other geographic variants are likely to be isolated in herpetoculture in the future and selectively bred. There often are consistencies in pattern and color of California kingsnakes from specific areas, allowing for a considerable degree of typing by herpetoculturists and segregation in breeding programs.

The color morphs are: normal phase color, characterized by varying degrees of light yellow bands or stripes; desert phase, distinguished by pure white bands or stripes; and at least three kinds of amelanistic albinos. Some of the albino morphs currently include standard albinos, lavender albinos with ruby-red eyes, and recently a lavender and bright yellow albino strain with red eyes.

Florida Kingsnake (*L. g. floridana*)

A good indicator of the Florida subspecies is the many crossbands of light scales that extend across the back. This subspecies is not often captive-bred. However, wild-caught specimens are regularly offered for sale. Actually, these snakes are heavily collected in the sugarcane fields south of Lake Okeechobee, where the large population is solely the result of humans' manipulation of the habitat in that area.

Florida kingsnakes are not widely bred in captivity.

These snakes are almost never collected from their natural habitat (glades, pinelands, and open grassland) because of the ease with which they are collected in the sugarcane fields. Recent genetic work now places the Florida kingsnake as a form of *L. g. getula*.

Eastern Kingsnake (*L. g. getula*)

The eastern kingsnake ranges from southern New Jersey to northern Florida. This subspecies is seldom captive-bred, but adults sometimes appear in pet or specialty stores. For the most part, this subspecies is uncommon in herpetoculture and becoming uncommon in the wild, mostly due to habitat destruction. Increased efforts need to be made to establish pure forms, not intergrades, in the trade. A black patternless specimen of the eastern kingsnake is currently in captivity and may become available in the future. This is the largest member of the genus, with an impressive record length of 84 inches (2.1 m).

The greatest concentration of these snakes occurs from Virginia to Georgia. Although these two states have protected them, neighboring North and South Carolina have not, and significant numbers continue to be collected

The eastern kingsnake is also called a chain kingsnake because its rings form a chainlike pattern along its body.

L. g. holbrooki's polka-dotted appearance makes it easy to see how it came by its common name, speckled kingsnake. The snake shown here resting on a branch exposes its ventral side, which is reduced in pattern.

there. The regular availability of wild-caught specimens may in part account for the general lack of interest in developing them for commercial herpetoculture.

Speckled Kingsnake (*L. g. holbrooki*)

Some specimens of speckled kingsnake, with its cream to yellow spot on each dark brown or brown scale, have a distinct greenish tint. This is a truly beautiful animal. Unfortunately, wild-caught specimens tend to be ill-tempered; captive-bred animals, however, which are usually available, prove to be good pets. An albino form has been developed by herpetoculturists and is regularly available. Its range is from southern Iowa to the Gulf of Mexico and west to eastern Texas.

Black Kingsnake (*L. g. nigra*)

Although this subspecies is referred to as the black kingsnake, it usually does have some pattern. This consists of greatly reduced light spots that may form slight bands across the back or just show a random light speckling down the back and sides. The ventral color is mostly black with intermittent white patches. The black kingsnake ranges from

Among herpetocultural trends regarding black kings, there is a preference toward pure black, such as seen here, rather than black with muted patterns.

southern Ohio down to central Alabama. This subspecies is rarely seen in pet stores and is even relatively uncommon in reptile specialty stores, either wild-caught or captive-bred. There are, however, several people in the United States who have successful breeding programs.

Mexican Black Kingsnake (*L. g. nigrita*)

The pure form (with no intergradation with other overlapping kingsnake subspecies) of the Mexican black kingsnake is usually all black or very dark brown, even to the scales on the underside. Hatchlings sometimes show a bit of a pattern, and the adults occasionally show some light spots along the sides. The Mexican black kingsnake's range is limited to northwestern Mexico and a small area in southern Arizona. Availability is still limited, although a number of herpetoculturists have had success breeding it.

This Mexican black king shows some light spots on the sides and carries the blue-eyed trait.

The desert king's natural habitat is the hot, dry areas of certain parts of Texas, New Mexico, and Arizona. To escape the high temperatures in these areas, this species is primarily nocturnal.

Desert Kingsnake (*L. g. splendida*)

This is the kingsnake that ranges from central Texas through southern and central New Mexico and into southern Arizona. It has a dark brown to black background color with numerous yellow or white spots on the sides. The light-colored scales form many thin bands across the back. Being from hot, dry areas, the desert kingsnake is normally nocturnal, although it can be found during the day near arroyos and dry washes after late spring rains. I have found this snake in southern Arizona in just such conditions. Wild-caught desert kingsnakes can frequently be found in local pet stores in the areas where they occur, but captive-bred babies are becoming more readily available to the general public.

No Longer Recognized Subspecies

There are some types of kingsnakes that were once recognized by herpetologists as separate subspecies but are no longer considered valid subspecies. *Lampropeltis getula* has been revised a number of times, with the most recent version favoring a reduction in the number of recognized subspecies. This is not to say that the unrecognized subspecies are not valued by herpeticulturists. To the contrary, these kingsnakes are highly prized and are being bred in their pure forms. Herpetoculturists place great emphasis on geographic and phenotypic variations of kingsnakes and have, in many cases, preserved the unique traits of various wild populations of all *Lampropeltis* species. This has been achieved through meticulous management of captive-bred populations. As a result, many herpetoculturists have chosen to retain subspecific names currently considered obsolete by the scientific community. This practice serves to represent and to segregate these distinctive *Lampropeltis* subspecies in the pet trade. In addition, the segregation of these morphs is desirable, especially when genetic lines from specific geographic areas are preserved (perhaps even ones threatened with destruction).

Note: To indicate that the unrecognized subspecies are herpetocultural forms rather than subspecies recognized in herpetology, I have chosen to list the herpetocultural subspecies in quotes.

South Florida Kingsnake (*L. g. "brooksi"*)

This kingsnake is considered by herpetologists to be only a variety of the Florida kingsnake (*L. g. floridana*). *"Brooksi"* is also known as the peninsula kingsnake and as the golden phase of the Florida kingsnake. A good *"brooksi"* has very little dark color to the scales, with most being tan to yellowish. There is almost no pattern in adults, although juveniles do show distinctive banding. This subspecies is found only in extreme southern Florida. It inhabits hammocks and glades as well as fields and can reach a length of 60 inches (1.5 m).

Note the reduced black pigment in this south Florida kingsnake (also called a Brook's or peninsula king) compared with the "true" Florida kingsnake *(L. g. floridana)*.

As is the case with the south Florida (Brook's) kingsnake, this blotched king (*L. g. "goini"*) is considered by herpetologists to be a subspecies of the "true" Florida kingsnake.

Blotched Kingsnake (*L. g. "goini"*)

Lampropeltis getula "goini" is known as the blotched kingsnake and only occurs in the Florida Panhandle (northwestern Florida) in the Chipola and Apalachicola River valleys. Herpetologists consider these kingsnakes to be *L. g. getula* and *L. g. floridana* intergrades (although recent work casts some doubt on this).

The bands are very wide, reduced in number, and composed of tan scales with dark dots in the middle of each one. The alternating dark bands may have tan dots in the middle of each scale. The effect is quite attractive. Adults can reach lengths of 60 inches (1.5 m). Herpetoculturists currently are breeding the following morphs: blotched, reverse patterned, patternless, and striped. Speckled and striped forms occur in nature. In fact, there is some well-founded speculation that these forms are the true *"goini"* and that the blotched form is an intergrade. The centuries of humans' impact on the habitat of these snakes, along with geographic transformation, may have allowed intergradation to occur.

In 2006, the name of this form was changed to *meansi*, the Apalachicola lowlands kingsnake, because of problems with the original description of *goini*. A few years later, however, *meansi* was declared a synonym of *L. g. floridana*. Hobbyists continue to use the name *"goini"* for this kingsnake.

Outer Banks Kingsnake (*L. g. "sticticeps"*)

The Outer Banks kingsnake is from the islands off the coast of North Carolina. It is distinguished by light-colored scales that form short bands across the back on a dark brown to black background. The bands do not extend around the body of the snake to meet the ventral scales. The top of the head and the labials (lip scales) usually have numerous white markings. Adults can reach a length of 50 inches (1.3 m). The Outer Banks kingsnake is an uncommon and beautiful snake that is rare in collections and is seldom available as a captive-bred animal.

It is believed that *L. g. "sticticeps"* is an intergrade between *L. g. getula* and *L. g. floridana*. However, it is well documented that *L. g. floridana* does not occur as far north as *getula*, so some speculated that this intergradation occurred in the distant past when *L. g. floridana* did range that far north. Others are skeptical of this theory. The newest genetic work confirms that *"sticticeps"* is a synonym of *L. g. getula*.

Yuma Kingsnake (*L. g. "yumensis"*)

This subspecies was once widely recognized. The wild-caught specimens found in its range (southwestern Arizona) superficially resemble the banded desert phase of *L. g. californiae*. The differences I have seen are that the bands are narrower and more numerous and there is much less white on the head. There is some conjecture that this is an intergrade between *L. g. californiae* and *L. g. splendida*.

Thinner bands distinguish the Yuma king from the California king. The Yuma specimen shown here was spotted near Tucson, Arizona.

CHAPTER 9

Prairie Kingsnakes and Milksnakes

I n addition to the common kingsnake species (*getula*), the kingsnake genus (*Lampropeltis*) comprises seven other species. Although these species vary in popularity and availability, they are kept and bred much as common kingsnakes are. This chapter and the two that follow discuss the appearances, locations, and general care of the species and major subspecies of these kings, the ones that usually are banded or at least spotted with red. These include the tricolored milksnakes and mountain kings as well as the interestingly patterned and colored gray-banded kings. One other species of kingsnake, the prairie king, is more closely related to the common kingsnake than to the other species. We will take a brief look at this species, before moving on to milksnakes.

Prairie Kingsnakes
(*Lampropeltis calligaster calligaster*)

The prairie king is found only in the eastern and central United States. A typical prairie king looks much like a dull corn snake (*Elaphe guttata*) or baby black rat snake (*E. obsoleta obsoleta*), but those species, unlike the prairie king, have weakly keeled scales over the spine and a divided anal scale. Typical prairie kings are grayish to tan, with fifty to seventy squarish dark brown blotches down the back. Adults seldom are more than 4 feet (1.2 m) long. A subspecies from the southeastern United States, the mole king (*Lampropeltis calligaster rhombomaculata*), tends to lose its pattern with age, becoming uniformly dark brown. The typical prairie king (*L. c. calligaster*), found from the Mississippi valley to west over the Great Plains, has a well-defined pattern in adults. The rare south Florida mole king (*L. c. occipitolineata*) looks more like a typical prairie king than

Although normal prairie kingsnakes (*L. c. calligaster*) are not especially popular, albino and striped specimens such as this one are sold widely for reasonable prices.

a mole king. Only the western prairie king is commonly found in the hobby, where it has been bred regularly. It often produces albino and striped morphs, which are very desirable.

Breeding and incubation of prairie kingsnake eggs are the same as for common kingsnake eggs. Females produce six to more than a dozen eggs, which hatch in forty-five to seventy-five days when incubated at 82°F–84°F (28°C–29°C). The young are brightly patterned and mature in two to three years.

Milksnakes
(*Lampropeltis triangulum*)

Many beginning hobbyists have a problem believing that milksnakes belong to the same group as California kingsnakes (*L. getula californiae*). Although the two have a similar body form, head scalation, and glossy body scales, the brilliant tricolored (red, black, and white or yellow) pattern of the milksnake is so different from the whitish yellow and black of the California king that it is easy to overlook the similarities.

In milksnakes, the typical pattern (excluding certain US subspecies) comprises rings of three colors in a consistent sequence: a black ring (or near ring) is bordered on either side by a whitish to yellowish or grayish ring; the black ring contains a red ring. The pattern thus runs: black-red-black-white-black-

69

The New Mexico milksnake (*L. t. celaenops*) displays the black-red-black-yellow pattern typical of most milksnakes, though the light-color ring varies from whitish to yellowish to grayish.

red-black-white. In some northern subspecies, the black and red colors appear as red blotches or saddles bordered at the front and back, and often to the lower sides, with black. In the northernmost subspecies, red is absent in many specimens, replaced by mahogany brown saddles edged by black on a gray to tan background, much like the coloration of a prairie kingsnake (*L. c. calligaster*) or a corn snake (*E. guttata*). In Central and South America, adults often are suffused with dark brown to black pigment and become almost all black.

Clearly, there is a great deal of variation in the milksnake—so much so that over the years some twenty-five subspecies have been named, with a combined range from southeastern Canada, across the eastern United States, west to about the Rockies, then south over much of Mexico, Central America, and northwestern South America. Many subspecies are defined more by statistics than by appearance (averages of numbers of white and red rings, for instance) and are difficult, if not impossible, to distinguish by general appearance. In fact, the concept of subspecies is questioned by many herpetologists, who suggest that the milksnake should be broken into three to five full species or the subspecies names ignored entirely. Because hobbyists and breeders identify snakes by subspecific names, we'll use them here.

Keeping Milksnakes

Unlike the other kingsnake species, which vary little in size or behavior, milksnakes fall into three categories: 1) small (less than 40 inches [1 m]), slender, northern subspecies that feed heavily on rodents; 2) very slender southeastern US snakes that feed mostly on lizards; and 3) longer (to more than 5 feet [1.5 m]), heavy-bodied snakes that feed on rodents. The major differences in keeping these types are in feeding the young and in vivarium size.

All milksnakes are nocturnal and do not need full-spectrum ultraviolet lights, although they may be added as many snakes will bask under them. All subspecies do well at about 60 to 80 percent relative humidity; those from tropical America (central Mexico to South America) often prefer the upper part of this range. Milks do not like high temperatures and are stressed when the thermometer rises above 86°F (30°C). They accept temperatures down to 75°F (24°C) well. Subspecies from the lowlands of tropical America do best at the higher temperatures; those from most of the United States and the highlands of tropical America can tolerate normal temperatures down to about 70°F (21°C). Provide a

Coral Snake Mimics

Any snake with alternating rings of red, black, and yellow may be called a coral snake mimic, including the milksnake. Many scientists feel that mimicry is not at work here because coral snakes are not found in the northern range of the milk. Rather, the coral snake-like patterns camouflage snakes that are active mostly at night, when red is visible as gray, and that move through the underbrush during the day, when the ringed pattern disappears against plant stems. Regardless, in the United States all milksnakes (and related harmless snakes with similar color patterns) have each red ring bordered on either side by black; the two species of coral snakes (genera *Micrurus* and *Micruroides*) have each red ring bordered by yellow.

temperature gradient in the vivarium. Small milksnake subspecies do well in vivaria or sweater boxes that are about 10-gallon (38-l) capacity; the largest tropical subspecies require at least a 30-gallon (114-l) vivarium. These strong snakes can climb up corners, so be sure that the lid locks securely. Every milk should have a secure hide box in which to disappear during the day. A shallow water bowl provides clean water for drinking, soaking, and easing the shedding process.

Shredded aspen, cypress mulch, and similar substrates work well on the cage bottom. If you use sand, be sure that damp foods are placed on a dry feeding plate to help prevent sand impactions of the snake's gut. Adult milksnakes (especially captive-bred specimens) will feed on thawed frozen mice of the appropriate size. Larger specimens will take adult mice or sometimes even rat pups; smaller subspecies take pinky to hopper mice. Most milks are excellent feeders in captivity, adjust well to handling, and make good pets.

Subspecies of the Milksnake

Although milksnake hobbyists and breeders recognize some two dozen subspecies, not all of them are commonly seen in the pet trade; a few are rare and almost never available as captive-bred specimens. Some subspecies are hard to distin-

Originating in northwestern Mexico but widely available in the United States now, the Sinaloan milksnake (*L. t. sinaloae*) is highly sought after for its bright, clean, and wide red rings.

guish from more popular subspecies and thus are not valued by hobbyists. More than half of the subspecies come from tropical regions in Mexico and Central America.

United States Subspecies

Of the US subspecies, a few are rare, but some are not brightly colored and thus not popular. Here is a look at six subspecies found in the United States, including the popular Mexican milksnake, which straddles the border between Texas and Mexico. See box on pages 74–75 for more subspecies.

Eastern Milksnake *(L. t. triangulum)*

The milksnake found from Minnesota to all over the north-eastern United States, and south to Kentucky, looks little like the other milksnakes. Typically, adults are slender snakes that may reach 4 to 5 feet (1.2 to 1.5 m) and have pale snouts. The pattern consists of oval brownish red to reddish blotches outlined with black and alternating down the center of the back, with small round spots on the lower sides.

There are no rings, not even behind the head, where the blotch on the nape sends branches onto the head like a broken arrowhead. The background color is tan. Juveniles

Eastern milksnakes (*L. t. triangulum*) vary considerably in color from one location to the next. Those snakes from the western part of the range are often brighter and more reddish than specimens such as this one from the eastern part.

73

tend to be brighter red than adults, but some adults keep quite a bit of color. The eastern milksnake feeds mostly on baby birds and rodents throughout its life. Because of its dull colors, the eastern milksnake is seldom offered commercially.

Red Milksnake (*L. t. syspila*)

Found from Indiana to North and South Dakota, and south to Oklahoma, the red milksnake is a popular and colorful little snake that forms a link between the eastern milksnake and the small subspecies from the

Subspecies of Milksnakes
The subspecies and their general ranges.

United States Forms

- Central plains milksnake, *L. t. gentilis*: central Texas north to Nebraska and eastern Colorado.
- Eastern milksnake, *L. t. triangulum*: Minnesota to New England, south to Kentucky.
- Louisiana milksnake, *L. t. amaura*: eastern Texas to Oklahoma to the Mississippi River.
- Mexican milksnake, *L. t. annulata*: southern Texas into northern Mexico.
- New Mexico milksnake, *L. t. celaenops*: southwestern Texas to New Mexico.
- Pale milksnake, *L. t. multistriata*: central Montana to Nebraska.
- Red milksnake, *L. t. syspila*: Indiana to the Dakotas, and south to Oklahoma.
- Scarlet kingsnake, *L. t. elapsoides*: Florida to Virginia and Tennessee.
- Utah milksnake, *L. t. taylori*: Utah to northern Arizona.

Mexican/Central American (Tropical) Forms

- Andean milksnake, *L. t. andesiana*: Colombia.
- Atlantic Central American milksnake, *L. t. polyzona*: northeastern Mexico, Atlantic Coast.

central United States. The pattern of the red milksnake is much like the pattern of an eastern milksnake, including oval blotches alternating with round spots on the sides, but the centers of the blotches are red or orange-red and the background color is white. There is a red ring at the back of the head; the snout generally is white.

Like other subspecies of milksnakes, the red milksnake varies considerably and also exchanges genes (intergrades) with adjacent subspecies, so individual specimens from the edges of its range are difficult to identify. This milksnake seldom reaches 30 inches (76 cm) in length.

- Black milksnake, *L. t. gaigeae*: Costa Rica and Panama.
- Blanchard's milksnake, *L. t. blanchardi*: Yucatán Peninsula, Mexico.
- Conant's milksnake, *L. t. conanti*: Guerrero and Oaxaca states, southern Mexico.
- Dixon's milksnake, *L. t. dixoni*: San Luis Potosi and Queretaro states, northeastern Mexico.
- Ecuadorian milksnake, *L. t. micropholis*: Panama to Colombia and Ecuador, low elevations.
- Guatemalan milksnake, *L. t. abnorma*: southeastern Mexico over northern Guatemala to Honduras.
- Honduran milksnake, *L. t. hondurensis*: eastern Honduras and Nicaragua to Costa Rica.
- Jalisco milksnake, *L. t. arcifera*: eastern-central Mexico.
- Nelson's milksnake, *L. t. nelsoni*: mostly Jalisco and Colima states, eastern Mexico.
- Pacific Central American milksnake, *L. t. oligozona*: southern Mexico to Honduras, Pacific Coast.
- Pueblan milksnake, *L. t. campbelli*: Puebla to Oaxaca states, southern Mexico.
- Sinaloan milksnake, *L. t. sinaloae*: northwestern Mexico.
- Smith's milksnake, *L. t. smithi*: San Luis Potosi to Veracruz states, Mexico.
- Stuart's milksnake, *L. t. stuarti*: Honduras to Costa Rica, Pacific Coast.

Central Plains Milksnake (*L. t. gentilis*)

As you go west and south from the range of the red milksnake, you find a variety of other subspecies that closely resemble it but lack the spots on the lower sides and have a more completely ringed pattern. These usually have black-specked white snouts and orange-red, black, and white rings. The most popular of these subspecies is the central plains milksnake, which is quite common from central Texas north to Nebraska and eastern Colorado. Few specimens are more than 3 feet (91 cm) long, and the overall appearance is of a slender snake with a small head. The whitish rings become tanner with age and may appear faintly yellowish in some specimens.

Louisiana Milksnake (*L. t. amaura*)

In this short (less than 2 feet [61 cm] long), slender milksnake, the pattern is typical of most milks from west of the Mississippi. It consists of relatively narrow black rings alternating with wide reddish rings, which often don't cross the belly, and somewhat narrower whitish rings (turning grayish with age). The snout is white. Although it is found in the Deep South from eastern Texas to Oklahoma and the Mississippi River, the Louisiana milksnake is most active during the late spring, before hot weather sets in. It frequently is found in rotting logs and stumps near lakes and bayous but also occurs in pinelands.

Hatchlings may insist on lizards for food and are difficult to start feeding. Widely sought, this snake is seldom common, but many captive-bred specimens in a variety of shades are available for dedicated hobbyists. In southern Louisiana, this subspecies seems to share genes with the scarlet kingsnake.

Scarlet Kingsnake (*L. t. elapsoides*)

The most fully banded and brightly colored US milksnake, this subspecies from Florida north to Virginia and Tennessee is considered the best coral snake mimic of the entire species. It has a bright red snout, wide red rings that cross the belly, and narrower black and yellow (white in hatchlings) rings

Many herpetologists believe the scarlet kingsnake (*L. t. elapsoides*) should be treated as a full species, *L. elapsoides*, because of its distinctive coloration and biology.

that also cross. The head and body are very slender, and adults seldom reach 20 inches (51 cm) long. Because scarlet kingsnakes look entirely different than some of the larger milksnakes from tropical America, many herpetologists believe these snakes should be considered a full species, *Lampropeltis elapsoides.*

Scarlet kingsnakes are very secretive, are not very common, and are not bred in large numbers. They have tiny hatchlings that may insist on skinks and other lizards for the first year of life. Some of these snakes never make the switch to mice. This is definitely a species better left to the experienced keeper.

Mexican Milksnake (*L. t. annulata*)

This beautiful milksnake technically could be considered a tropical subspecies that ranges southern Texas into northern Mexico rather than a US subspecies. Although smaller than many tropical forms (seldom more than 30 inches [76 cm] long), it is rather heavy bodied, with a large, mostly black head. The body is ringed with black, yellow to white, and red. The red rings number fourteen to twenty. This is a subspecies of relatively dry areas, frequently found near lakes and rivers. It is quite popular, easy to keep, and widely available.

Mexican and Central American (Tropical) Subspecies

Most milksnakes in Mexico and Central America look much like the Mexican milksnake and form a bewildering tangle of difficult-to-identify subspecies not especially common or popular in the hobby. Four subspecies, however, are quite distinct and very popular.

Pueblan Milksnake (*L. t. campbelli*)

In the Pueblan milk from southern Mexico, the stark white rings are exceptionally wide, often wider than the red rings; the black rings also may be very wide. Although the snout and head in front of the eyes are black, there is a wide white ring over the rest of the head and the nape. At first glance, the Pueblan milk looks like a white milksnake with red and black rings, and captive-bred specimens often accentuate the white even more. The snout is quite short, the head wide, and the body heavy. Specimens may reach 3 feet (91 cm) in length. The Pueblan milksnake is now widely available.

Sinaloan Milksnake (*L. t. sinaloae*)

If you like bright red, this is the milksnake for you. Typical specimens (captive-bred specimens now come in a variety of shades and patterns) have a black head and snout, with a narrow white ring at the back, and white or yellow and black rings that are relatively narrow and of about the same width. There are only ten to sixteen red rings, these being about three times the width of the black-yellow-black grouping. The red is clear, without black speckling. With captive breeding, the black and white rings sometimes become reduced in extent and may appear as just spots or broken bands, resulting in a mostly red milksnake. This is a big (4 feet [1.2 m] long), heavy-bodied milksnake with a large head. Unlike other tropical milks, this subspecies comes from dry habitats, in northwestern Mexico.

Honduran Milksnake (*L. t. hondurensis*)

This big (often more than 4 feet [1.2 m] long), heavy-bodied, blunt-headed tropical milksnake—which comes from

Breeders have produced many variations of the popular Honduran milksnake (*L. t. hondurensis*), from specimens that virtually lack red, such as the one shown here, to those that are almost uniformly red.

eastern Honduras, Nicaragua, and Costa Rica—started out as a typically ringed milk with narrow yellow rings, moderately wide black rings, and about fourteen to twenty-six red rings nearly as wide as the black-yellow-black groups. The snout is black, often followed by a yellow band.

However, most Honduran milks for sale are not the natural color. Captive breeding of wild snakes from different sources has produced at least a dozen major color morphs, from pure white to almost uniformly red, with just traces of black pigment. Tangerine Hondurans have the yellow rings replaced with wide salmon to orange rings that, through selective breeding, have become as red as the true red rings, with the black rings often reduced. In morphs that lack the black pigment (amelanistic albinos), the red and yellow pigments become incredibly bright. In those lacking the red and yellow pigments (anerythristic albinos), wide white bands are sharply separated from wide black bands. Many breeders and keepers specialize in Hondurans, and new varieties are bred each year. These can be nervous snakes; if two are kept together, one may be killed during feeding accidents.

Black Milksnake (*L. t. gaigeae*)

Although uncommon and expensive, this exceptional subspecies of the milksnake deserves mention. Coming from the highlands of Costa Rica and Panama, where the air and ground temperatures remain cool all year, these snakes

Although young black milksnakes (*L. t. gaigeae*) are tricolored like other milks, adults usually are uniformly glossy black, as is this one.

darken with age, presumably to help them absorb heat and stay warm enough for activity. Like many other tropical milks, black milksnake hatchlings are ringed with black, yellow, and wide red bands; as the snakes mature, however, brownish pigment begins to hide the original pattern. Adults are uniformly blackish brown above and below, without a trace of pattern. These are big milks that may exceed 5 feet (1.5 m) and are very heavy bodied. They tend to be nervous when handled and are kept mostly as a novelty by specialists. The other milks from the far southern edge of the range of *L. t. gaigeae* (*L. t. micropholis* [Ecuadorian milk], found in Panama, Colombia, and Ecuador; and *L. t. andesiana* [Andean milk], found in Columbia) also tend to be large, heavy-bodied snakes, with a lot of black in the red rings. Juveniles of the two subspecies look much like young black milks.

Breeding Milksnakes

Like other kingsnakes, milksnakes breed after coming out of a winter cooling, during which they are kept at 50°F–60°F (10°C–16°C), with reduced light and no food, just water. For subspecies from the United States, most are cooled for about three months at nearly 50°F (10°C), but tropical subspecies do best at 60°F (16°C) for just two months. The snakes should be caged separately and slowly returned to normal maintenance temperatures in the early spring. After a few meals, the sexes are put together and should mate (usually at night) within a few days to a few weeks. Females generally lay four to twelve

A Pueblan milksnake (*L. t. campbelli*) coils about her clutch of eggs. The eggs should hatch in approximately eight weeks.

large, oval, white eggs, which are incubated at 79°F–82°F (26°C–28°C) on moist vermiculite or sphagnum moss in a container that maintains about 100 percent relative humidity. The eggs hatch in approximately two months.

Hatchlings of the larger subspecies generally take live pinky mice as soon as they go through their first shed, then will quickly grow to take adult mice. The small, slender subspecies, however, may be difficult to raise because the hatchlings are so small, with very small heads. Often you must resort to offering baby skinks or house geckos (*Hemidactylus turcicus*) or even just the lizards' tails to get the young feeding. As often is the case with small hatchlings, some will not feed until the following spring, and some never feed. This is why beginning keepers often do better breeding the larger tropical milksnakes than the more common US subspecies.

CHAPTER 10

Mountain Kingsnakes

L ike the milksnake, the two species of mountain king-snakes are beautifully marked, tricolored snakes, with numerous triads of black-red-black separated by pale bands. In both mountain kings, the pale bands are white or sometimes grayish white but never yellow; the red varies from brilliant scarlet to orange-red.

Keeping Mountain Kingsnakes

Both mountain kingsnakes are notoriously secretive. They are nocturnal feeders in nature, and their normal diet in the wild consists of lizards, small mammals, and birds. These king-snakes tend to be found at moderate elevations in mountains and canyons covered with junipers, pines, and similar trees, and they spend their days under logs and rocks, sometimes coming out to bask in weak sunlight. They are most likely active after rains from spring through autumn.

The Sonoran mountain kingsnake (*Lampropeltis pyromelana*), shown above, is one of two species of mountain kingsnakes; the other is the California mountain kingsnake (*Lampropeltis zonata*). Both species are small, beautifully colored, and secretive.

In practice, this means that mountain kingsnakes prefer relatively small cages with hiding places, where they can escape from the light. A specimen is kept singly as a rule (remember that accidents can happen during feeding and one snake could swallow another) in a vivarium of about a 10-gallon (38-l) capacity, with a thick layer of aspen mulch; a rock pile, a hide box, or a piece of cork in one corner; a stable water bowl; and a feeding bowl. A mountain kingsnake does not need a full-spectrum basking light, although it doesn't hurt to provide one in case a specimen feels like basking during the day. A relative humidity between 50 and 70 percent should be fine.

Mountain kingsnakes do not tolerate high temperatures. Provide a temperature gradient from 65°F (18°C) in the coolest corner to 79°F (26°C) in the warmest. An under-tank heating pad or heat tapes work best. Higher temperatures can be stressful, even deadly; at much lower temperatures, the snakes will not feed or be active. During the winter, most snakes become inactive and will retreat to the coolest corner, so the temperature of the entire vivarium can be dropped.

These are small snakes that usually take relatively small prey. Like other kingsnakes, they are constrictors. Most specimens (especially captive-breds) will quickly adapt to taking pinky to hopper mice fed in the evening. Some will insist on lizards as food at first but will eventually adapt to mice. Mountain kingsnakes are known to stop feeding in autumn and may not feed again until the following summer. Captive-bred specimens are usually good feeders, especially when overwintered at cool temperatures without food.

Sonoran Mountain Kingsnake
(Lampropeltis pyromelana)

The Sonoran mountain kingsnake is slender bodied and has more than forty white rings separating the triads; its snout is all white. It is found at moderately high elevations in dry mountains from central Utah, to over much of Arizona, and southward into Sonora and Chihuahua, Mexico. Although the kingsnakes from each mountain range look a bit different, herpetologists have been unsure how to classify them. Certain herpetologists have recognized four subspecies, others have recognized three.

However, a new understanding of genetics and variation in Sonoran mountain kingsnake populations shows that the traditional subspecies cannot be recognized, so the species stands as just *L. pyromelana* without subspecies. In addition, the Chihuahua mountain kingsnake, once categorized as a Sonoran subspecies, is now considered a full species, *L. knoblochi*, whose range extends north into southern Arizona. This change most likely will be accepted in the hobby literature.

Despite the scientific evidence, however, subspecies of *L. pyromelana* are still discussed in the hobby and can be found in both present and older works. To aid the reader, here are the so-called subspecies as described in other works.

Utah Mountain Kingsnake
(*L. p. infralabialis*)

The Utah mountain kingsnake is considered the northernmost form of the Sonoran mountain king, being found in central Utah southward into northern Arizona around the Grand Canyon. It has only nine scales (infralabials) on each side of the lower jaw; the other populations of the species have ten. Remember, however, that this is an average over a long series of specimens, and individual specimens may vary. Additionally, the Utah mountain kingsnake has forty-two to fifty-seven white rings between the triads, with half or more extending completely around the body.

Arizona Mountain Kingsnake
(*L. p. pyromelana*)

In the Arizona mountain kingsnake, there are forty-one or more white rings between the triads; fewer than half of the white rings cross the belly completely. There are ten infralabial scales in normal specimens. This kingsnake is found in many mountain ranges from central Arizona into northern Sonora and Chihuahua in Mexico.

Even before a new understanding of genetics showed that the Sonoran mountain king has no subspecies, the Huachuca mountain kingsnake's classification as *L. p. woodini* was seriously questioned, and few people recognized it as a true subspecies.

Huachuca Mountain Kingsnake
(*L. p. woodini*)

Very similar to the Arizona mountain kingsnake is the Huachuca mountain kingsnake, which is restricted to the Huachuca Mountains area of southern Arizona and northern Sonora. In theory, *L. p. woodini* has only thirty-seven to forty white rings around the body, fewer than in the adjacent *L. p. pyromelana*. The problem is that the number of bands varies greatly in mountain kings throughout Arizona. It is not uncommon to find snakes fitting the description of *woodini* even in central Arizona; some looking like typical *pyromelana* are found in the Huachuca Mountains. This has led to the conclusion that the subspecies *woodini* should not be recognized.

Chihuahua Mountain Kingsnake
(*L. p. knoblochi*)

Perhaps even more desirable in the hobby today than Arizona or Utah specimens of the Sonoran mountain king are specimens of the Chihuahua mountain kingsnake, which came originally from an isolated region of Chihuahua, Mexico. Once very rare (Mexico seldom allows legal exportation of this or other kingsnakes), the Chihuahua mountain kingsnake has been bred in captivity for perhaps two decades and now is

Formerly categorized as a subspecies of the Sonoran mountain king-snake (*L. pyromelana*), the Chihuahua mountain kingsnake is now considered its own species, *L. knoblochi*. This once-rare snake from a remote region of northern Mexico is widely bred in captivity today.

widely available, although expensive. As originally described, there are about seventy triads bearing wide, red, squarish saddles that almost never extend all the way to the belly. Instead, the red is bordered at the lower edges by a white line and then by a jagged black line where colored bands have come up from the belly and are partially fused into lines. In captive-bred specimens, however, the extent of red has increased, and although still not extending to the belly, the red now typically looks much like the bands of the other subspecies. Colors vary from bright red to orange-red, with glossy white to grayish white bands. Breeders recognize several distinct captive-bred lines as the result of different ancestors and selective breeding.

Breeding Sonoran Mountain Kingsnakes

Because of the bright colors of the Sonoran mountain kings, many keepers have tried to breed them—with mixed results. Some keepers' snakes produce young every season; others' never succeed. One problem is that some males are not fertile. If a pairing doesn't work for two years, try changing the male, or better yet, put the female with two or three males in turn.

Offer no food after the beginning of November (most snakes stop feeding naturally by this time anyway) so the gut will be entirely empty. Slowly drop the temperature from a high of near 79°F (26°C) down to 50°F (10°C) over the next two weeks, and hold it there. It is important that the snakes be given a proper cooling period during the winter so the sperm can mature and the snakes can get into breeding condition. The snakes will become inactive but do not truly hibernate, as they still will move around their cages a bit and will drink. Make sure that water is always available. House snakes separately. After three months of this low temperature, turn the heat on, and over the next week to two weeks return the vivaria to normal. Make sure there is water for the snakes to soak in if desired. Within a week or two, the snakes should start feeding normally, and the male will spend much of his time searching for the female. Once the snakes have had one or two meals, put them together. Keep the pair together for a month or two, then remove the male.

Females begin to swell within a month of a successful mating, and they will lay within two months of mating. A gravid female generally molts about two weeks before laying. The clutch consists of just two to six eggs on average; the eggs are very large, white, and oval. Incubate the eggs at 82°F (28°C) in vermiculite (one part water to one part vermiculite by weight) for approximately fifty-five to seventy days. The babies will be very slender, with small heads, and will not feed until after their first molts in one to two weeks. Babies may require lizard tails or pinky mouse parts as their first meals. It may be necessary to scent mice or mouse parts with lizard skin or intestinal contents before they are eaten. You can expect some loss of babies, but don't give up on those that are not feeding. They may go a full season without doing so, taking their first meals after the first winter cooling period.

California Mountain Kingsnakes
(*Lampropeltis zonata*)

California mountain kingsnakes are restricted to the mountains from northwestern Mexico to Washington State. These are fairly heavy-bodied snakes, with more than thirty, but typically fewer than forty, stark white rings between the triads. The triads themselves often consist of two completely fused black bands with at most two red spots within. In this mountain kingsnake, the snout is always black, which may lead some people to think this is a milksnake. These kings have a few more white bands than do milksnakes, however, and the white bands usually don't widen as they approach the belly, remaining a constant width on the lower sides. In many California mountain kingsnakes, the triads are incomplete, with the red broken over the spine by a wide black intrusion from the black bands on either side. Often the red is restricted to large or small spots in the lower part of a triad, and sometimes red is entirely absent from the pattern. Typical California mountain kings have nine lower labial scales (ten in Sonoran mountain kings from most of Arizona and Mexico). Few specimens are much more than 30 inches (76 cm) long.

It is especially difficult to define subspecies in *Lampropeltis zonata* because there is great variation among local populations and even individuals within a small area. Traditionally, herpetologists have recognized as many as seven subspecies based on tendencies toward different numbers of triads and development of red in the pattern, but this has been seriously challenged in modern studies. Because keepers often use traditional subspecific names, let's summarize them here before going into the subspecies problem. The subspecies are treated from north to south.

Captive-bred specimens are your best bet as they feed more reliably than wild-caught specimens do and are almost certain to be legal. Because of the desirability of these snakes and the misguided efforts of some collectors who destroy rock piles when collecting the snakes, California and Oregon have put severe restrictions on collecting, breeding, and even owning this species. Mexico does not allow exportation of its forms without special permits, which seldom are issued.

St. Helena Mountain Kingsnake (*L. z. zonata*) and Sierra Mountain Kingsnake (*L. z. multicincta*)

The St. Helena mountain kingsnake is one of two subspecies in which the wide white ring at the back of the head is entirely behind the angle of the jaw. In 60 percent

The subspecies of the California mountain kingsnake found south of San Francisco along the coast is *L. z. multifasciata*, the coastal mountain kingsnake. This small, colorful subspecies commonly has solid red rings extending completely across the back.

or more of the triads, the red band is broken into two large blotches by black along the spine. This is one of the larger of the subspecies, with adults commonly 30 or more inches (76 cm) long. *L. z. zonata* is restricted in its pure form to the mountains north of San Francisco Bay.

The Sierra mountain kingsnake is virtually identical to the St. Helena subspecies but has more complete red bands in the triads, with fewer than 60 percent of the triads broken on the spine by black. *L. z. multicincta* is found in its pure form in the Sierra Nevada range of northern and eastern California.

Other California Mountain Kingsnakes

Specimens of California mountain kings from coastal ranges in northern California and southwestern Oregon (as well as an isolated population that can be found in southern Washington) appear to be intergrades between the St. Helena and Sierra mountain kingsnakes. Curiously, the intergrades have a wide range outside the contact zone of the subspecies, which has long led scientists to question the validity of the subspecies.

Many small and fragmented populations of mountain kings occur in the coastal ranges from San Francisco Bay south into northern Baja California, Mexico. These have been broken into five subspecies that are especially variable and hard to define.

The **coastal mountain kingsnake** (*L. z. multifasciata*) is the form found from San Francisco to Ventura County, California. *L. z. multifasciata* frequently has red mottling on the snout and is small, with fewer than forty-one triads bordered by narrow black bands, the red being wide and bright. The wide white band at the back of the head touches the angle of the jaws. Since most specimens lack black intrusions into the red along the spine, this is an especially colorful subspecies.

San Diego mountain kingsnakes (*L. z. pulchra*) have only thirty-two or so triads, and the red bands are widely interrupted by black in only 30 percent of the triads. This is a small and rather slender subspecies of California mountain kingsnake, with the snout black and the white head band over the angle of the jaws. These kings are found from Los Angeles to San Diego County in California, frequently along the coast.

San Bernardino mountain kingsnakes (*L. z. parvirubra*) are much like the San Diego subspecies, but they are found in mountains of the interior ranges from west of Los Angeles to Riverside County, California. There are thirty-five or more triads, and in many of the triads (less than 60 percent), the red band is not broken by black on the spine.

In the San Pedro Martir and Sierra Juarez Mountains of northern Baja California is found the **San Pedro** or **Baja California mountain kingsnake** (*L. z. agalma*), a form that can no longer be imported legally but has been widely captive-bred. About half the forty-plus triads are mostly black, with red restricted to small blotches low in the triad; some specimens have very little red. Few specimens are more than 24 inches (61 cm) long.

Seldom seen is the **Todos Santos mountain kingsnake** (*L. z. herrerae*), which comes only from a small island off the northwestern coast of Baja California. In this form, the red is virtually absent from the pattern, the snake being white with black bands across the back, much like a California kingsnake (*L. getula californiae*). If red is present, it usually takes the form of small spots low on the sides or faintly pink bands within the triads. Few specimens are much more than 2 feet (61 cm) long.

Lampropeltis Zonata Clades

Unfortunately, these many subspecies seem to have little reality in nature (they exist more in the minds of collectors and some herpetologists than as natural, consistent genetic subspecies). Individual specimens from almost any part of the range may look like specimens of other subspecies. Recent DNA studies show that the species is better split into two ancestral groups (clades): one north of Los Angeles (with two distinguishable forms within it, about equivalent to *L. z. zonata* to the north and in the Sierra Nevadas and *L. z. multifasciata* between San Francisco and Los Angeles) and one to the south (roughly equivalent to *L. z. agalma*). Although scientists are likely to adopt this scheme, breeders still prefer to use the other names to help indicate the origin of the parents.

Breeders still divide the California mountain kingsnake (*Lampropeltis zonata*) into subspecies, such as the San Pedro mountain king (*L. z. agalma*) seen here. DNA studies show that the species is better split into two ancestral groups, one roughly equivalent to *L. z. agalma*.

Breeding California Mountain Kingsnakes

Although many California mountain kings come from relatively dry, warm areas of southern California and northwestern Mexico, most are found in dry mountains at significant elevations that become quite cold during the winter. This means that breeding is most likely to occur following a winter cooling period. Many California mountain kings stop feeding during the autumn; this can be used as a signal to remove all food over a period of two weeks and begin cooling the vivarium. Slowly drop the temperature from its maximum of about 79°F (26°C) to about 50°F (10°C), and hold that temperature for three months. Provide a water bowl during this time, but keep the vivarium dark. Check frequently to make sure that the snakes (which usually are housed separately) are healthy and not dehydrating or developing fungal or bacterial infections. Usually, the cooling period starts around late November in the United States, and the snakes are slowly brought back to normal temperatures over two weeks starting in February.

As the temperature gets back to normal, the snakes should start feeding heavily and may soak and molt. A month or two after cooling stops, put the sexes together; expect mating to take place at night. Males may show reduced fertility in captivity, so after two or three unsuccessful breeding seasons, you should consider switching males or putting a female with two or three different males over a few weeks.

Females lay a clutch of two to six large, oval, white eggs that hatch in sixty to seventy-five days when incubated at 82°F (28°C). Commonly, vermiculite (one part vermiculite to one part water by weight) is used for the incubation substrate. As with the Sonoran mountain kingsnake, excessive humidity during incubation can kill the eggs. Baby California mountain kingsnakes are very slender, delicate snakes with small heads. Difficult feeders may have to be started on lizards. Both the Sonoran and California mountain kingsnakes may live fifteen to twenty years in captivity.

CHAPTER 11

Gray-Banded Kingsnakes

Found from southwestern Texas into central Mexico in dry, rocky country, the two species of gray-banded kingsnakes (*Lampropeltis mexicana* and *L. alterna*) are closely related to another species, Ruthven's kingsnake (*Lampropeltis ruthveni*), from a bit farther south in Mexico. The three species are rather stout-bodied, wide-headed kings, seldom more than 3 feet (91 cm) long. In the three species, a common (although not necessarily typical) pattern consists of pairs of black bands across the back split by a red to orange-red spot, blotch, or band; these triads are separated by the grayish background color. The red can be absent or form wide regular bands extending onto the belly. At one extreme (typical *L. alterna*) are specimens that are metallic gray with narrow black bands alternating with rows of large black spots, having little or no red present. The most extreme patterns include broad red bands separated by narrow black bands and pale grayish white bands, almost identical, even on close examination, to those of some milksnakes. There is much individual and populational variation in the snakes, and the different species and patterns have been interbred in captivity, then selectively bred to produce special color patterns.

Although most scientists do agree that Ruthven's kingsnake is a full species (but confusingly similar to the milksnake in many aspects), *Lampropeltis mexicana* and *L. alterna* are extremely similar and are thought to intergrade in Mexico, so some herpetologists believe they are subspecies of a single species. However, most hobbyists today prefer to restrict the common name "gray-banded kingsnake" to the Texas species (*L. alterna*), while calling the gray-band found in central Mexico the Mexican kingsnake (*L. mexicana*). The following summary treats these kings as full species with several color variants.

Texas Gray-Banded Kingsnakes (*Lampropeltis alterna*)

Found in the Big Bend area of southwestern Texas, barely into New Mexico, and in adjacent Mexico, the Texas gray-banded kingsnake is one of the most popular and sought-after kingsnakes today. Although widely bred in captivity, it is still collected regularly by breeders who want to find their own specimens at night in remote Texas canyons. It is nocturnal, not especially common, and restricted to the narrow breaks and gaps in the walls of dry canyons and road cuts mostly west of the Pecos River. During the day, *L. alterna* lives underground, feeding primarily on lizards. It sometimes comes out at night and crosses roads or can be found on the sides of canyons. Breeders try to accumulate specimens from specific localities, although color patterns are not restricted to any particular locality.

Typical gray-banded kingsnakes are wide headed, with protruding eyes, and are metallic gray or bluish gray. There is little or no red in the pattern (although sometimes small

Although most of the body of this hatchling Texas gray-banded kingsnake (*L. alterna*) shows a colorful *blairi*-phase pattern, the front of the body has an odd striped and spotted pattern. Such anomalies may start distinctive lines of color variations.

red blotches may interrupt the black bands or appear on the nape of the neck), which consists of narrow black bands alternating with rows of two or more black spots. If there is a blotch on the nape, it is located well behind the head. Although not especially colorful, well-marked specimens are quite interesting. It has been suggested that the pattern mimics that of the local rock rattlesnake, *Crotalus lepidus*.

The *blairi* phase of *L. alterna* looks like a totally different snake and was first described as a full species, *Lampropeltis blairi*. It now is known to occur in the same localities as typical gray-bands and may hatch out from clutches of eggs taken from gray-banded females, so it has no taxonomic standing. Typical specimens are blue-gray, with about fourteen wide orange-red saddles on the back outlined with black.

Mexican Kingsnakes (*Lampropeltis mexicana*)

Found in northern and central Mexico, this species looks much like a gray-banded kingsnake but usually has irregular black-edged reddish blotches down the back and a large reddish blotch on the head itself (rather than just on the nape).

Mexican kingsnakes (*L. mexicana*) are gray-banded kingsnakes that show many different patterns. This colorful Mexican king has a fairly typical *thayeri*-phase pattern that resembles the pattern of a milksnake at first glance.

Although Mexican kingsnakes are very colorful, the typical phase is not widely bred. The species shows even more variation than does *L. alterna*. Breeders commonly sell three other types of patterns.

The *greeri* phase (once described as a full species, *L. greeri*) also is called the Durango kingsnake. The blotches on the back are reduced in size and widely separated by a blue-gray background color. Commonly, the blotches take the form of blackish brown circles or narrow bands with reddish centers.

The *thayeri* phase (again once described as a full species, *L. thayeri*) takes two forms in captivity. One is the milksnake pattern, which has broad reddish bands narrowly edged with black that extend to the edge of the belly. More commonly seen, however, is the melanistic pattern, which is uniformly blackish brown from snout to tail tip.

Ruthven's Kingsnake
(*Lampropeltis ruthveni*)

This heavy-bodied milksnake-like king—also called the Queretaro kingsnake from the Mexican state where breeding

Most specimens of Ruthven's kingsnake (*L. ruthveni*) are sold as beautiful albinos, with red eyes and no trace of black in the pattern. Some specimens have cleaner, brighter colors than others and sell at a premium.

stock was originally collected—has broad bright red bands encircling the body, edged by wide black bands; narrow straw to grayish bands separate the triads. The head is black with reddish specks and blotches, and there is a narrow pale band behind the jaws.

Today you are more likely to find albino Ruthven's kings for sale than you are to find typical specimens. These gorgeous albinos usually are glossy white and lavender pink, with brilliant red bands. Albino Ruthven's kings have been interbred with *L. alterna* to produce an albino strain in the latter species.

Breeding Gray-Banded Kingsnakes

These kingsnakes are more difficult to breed than are common kingsnakes, but like common kingsnakes, they generally require a cooling period of about three months at 55°F (13°C) to mate successfully. Breeders often drop the temperature over a period of two weeks, making sure the snakes have empty guts when they reach the low point. Cooling is easiest from mid-December through mid-March. Clutches number from five to a dozen or more large white eggs that hatch in roughly fifty to seventy days at 82°F (28°C). The young are small and delicate and may refuse to feed on pinky mice. Many young are lost, but most can be persuaded to take gecko tails, pinky tails and legs, or pinkies rubbed with lizard scent. Once they start eating, they are hardy snakes that can be housed like common kingsnakes.

Resources

Conant, R., and J. T. Collins. 1998. 4th edition. *A field guide to reptiles and amphibians: Eastern and Central North America.* Boston: Houghton Mifflin.

Dunham, T. 2002. Banded beauties. *Reptiles* 10(9): 52–73.

Frost, D. R., and J. T. Collins. 1988. Nomenclatural notes on reptiles of the United States. *Herpetological Review* 19(4): 73–74.

Fry, F. 1991. *Reptile care.* Vols. 1 & 2. Neptune City, NJ: TFH Publications.

Markel, R. G. 1990. *Kingsnakes and milksnakes.* Neptune City, NJ: TFH Publications.

Mattison, C. 1999. *Keeping and breeding snakes.* 2nd edition. New York: Sterling Publishing.

Mills, T. 1989. To scent or not to scent. *Vivarium* 2(3): 8–10, 27.

Stebbins, R. C. 2003. 3rd edition. *A field guide to western reptiles and amphibians.* Boston: Houghton Mifflin.

Wright, A. H., and A. A. Wright. 1957. *Handbook of snakes of the United States and Canada.* Ithaca, NY: Comstock.

Index

99

About the Authors

A graduate of University of South Florida with a bachelor's degree in zoology, **David Perlowin** has pursued various herpetological breeding projects over the years and is also the author of *Garter Snakes and Water Snakes* (I-5 Press, 2nd ed., 2005). Today David spends most of his time on a different vocation—the art of watchmaking. A second-generation watchmaker, David, who lives in Santa Fe, New Mexico, with his wife, Paula, runs a business restoring vintage timepieces.

A native of central Louisiana, **Jerry G. Walls** worked as an editor in New Jersey for more than thirty years, authoring more than 400 publications on natural history subjects, especially reptiles and amphibians. He edited *Reptile Hobbyist* magazine and has written more than forty books about various animals. Jerry teaches biology at Louisiana State University, Alexandria.

The Experts At
Advanced Vivarium Systems®
Present
The Herpetocultural Library®

The most comprehensive and precise information available for the care and breeding of your reptiles.

Learn all the secrets from the experts. You'll find special tips and advice along with fundamental information, detailed with the accuracy that our readers have come to expect ONLY from The Herpetocultural Library Series®. Learn the techniques necessary for proper maintenance, breeding, feeding, housing, lighting, temperature requirements, supplementation, incubation, and the rearing of juveniles. You'll also find sections on disease and treatments, various morphs, and more!